RISE OF THE DATA CLOUD

AuthorHouse™
1663 Liberty Drive
Bloomington, IN 47403
www.authorhouse.com
Phone: 1 (833) 262-8899

Because of the dynamic nature of the Internet, any web addresses or links contained in this book may have changed since publication and may no longer be valid. The views expressed in this work are solely those of the author and do not necessarily reflect the views of the publisher, and the publisher hereby disclaims any responsibility for them.

This book is printed on acid-free paper.

Photographs © Bill Roberts
Cover images: Shutterstock, Inc.

ISBN: 978-1-7283-6360-8 (sc)
ISBN: 978-1-7283-7306-5 (e)

Library of Congress Control Number: 2020918986

Printed in the United States of America.

Published by AuthorHouse 10/12/2020

authorHOUSE®

RISE

OF THE

DATA

CLOUD

FRANK SLOOTMAN

CEO OF SNOWFLAKE

and STEVE HAMM

CONTENTS

Top View   1

FRANK SLOOTMAN

CONTENTS

RISE OF THE DATA CLOUD

TOP VIEW

An Introduction

_____

FRANK SLOOTMAN

I N THE SPRING of 2019, I was living the retired CEO life with my wife, Brenda, at our place in Pleasanton, California, when I got an email from Mike Speiser, a venture capitalist I had known for years. He wrote that he wanted to catch up. From time to time, Mike and I would have lunch in the East Bay or on the Peninsula. We would discuss his companies as well as broader things happening in the industry.

In recent years, Mike had spoken enthusiastically about Snowflake, while at the same time noting that the young company needed help. In that vein, he had suggested that I consider joining the board. Nothing ever came of that, and I did not think any more about it.

This time, Mike got straight to the point: "What would it take for you to take the helm at Snowflake?" He was asking me to become CEO of one of the hottest tech companies in Silicon Valley.

Snowflake was at the time a seven-year-old company that had raised more than $929 million in venture funding and had a valuation of $4 billion. It was a true Silicon Valley unicorn. (In February 2020, the company raised an additional $479 million, giving it a market valuation of $12.4 billion. By then, it had thousands of customers.)

I was taken aback at first. I had made it abundantly clear to anybody who asked that I was not considering taking the field anytime soon, if ever again. I had for two years avoided conversations like this. I was retired, full stop.

Now, though, I was intrigued.

Mike was the founding venture capitalist at Snowflake and had served as CEO for nearly two years before Bob Muglia, a former top Microsoft executive, took over. Bob was a good match for Snowflake's small but potent team, which included technologist founders Benoit Dageville, Thierry Cruanes, and Marcin Zukowski. Together, they developed Snowflake into a bantamweight fighter capable of duking it out with tech industry heavyweights Amazon, Google, Microsoft, Oracle, and Teradata.

Mike led Snowflake during its infancy. Bob led it through adolescence. And I was offered the chance to lead the company to become a mature adult.

Long story short, I took the job.

WHY I JOINED SNOWFLAKE

In my view, the founders had struck a chord with Snowflake. Anybody who got close to the product was mesmerized by its scale, performance, and utter simplicity. This was not some incrementally better product. It had the potential to reimagine data management for the cloud. The founders had burned the ships behind them, too. They decided early on to operate only in the public cloud, not "on premises" in customers' data centers. That made no sense to them.

Snowflake focused on the struggle that organizations face in processing what is known as Big Data—collections of data large enough to overwhelm most commercially available computing systems. Over the years, so-called data warehousing companies had emerged with proprietary computer hardware designed to increase the scale of data processing. Clusters of computers are connected so they behave like a single computer. Companies such as Teradata and Netezza popularized this approach. But these systems had major drawbacks. They were super-expensive, out of reach for all but the largest enterprises. In addition, even they had significant scale and performance limits.

IT managers responsible for running corporate data centers (on-premises computing) tell horror stories of struggling to get the performance they needed out of their systems. Randy Wigginton, director of platform engineering at Square, recalls that he was under constant stress—so much so that one day he had to go to the hospital because of heart palpitations. Randy has seen it all and done it all during his long career in the computer industry. He was employee No. 6 at Apple and later worked at E-Trade, eBay, and Google. But Big Data nearly did him in. (Square later became a Snowflake customer.)

Meanwhile, open source technologies such as Hadoop, developed by the Apache Software Foundation, have also taken on the challenges of Big Data. Hadoop was popularized and supported by firms including Cloudera and MapR. While these techniques helped with scale, they also introduced vast complexity, which limited the technology's appeal.

In short, the incumbents were expensive, limited on scale and performance, and highly complex. At the same time, the growth and importance of data continued to jump off the charts, making it glaringly obvious that the status quo could not last.

Enter Snowflake. Its architecture raised the data scale from terabytes to petabytes, a thousandfold increase, and reduced task execution times from days and hours to minutes and seconds. It was so simple to use that anybody with a rudimentary knowledge of SQL (Structured Query Language), the most common database query language, could get up and running with Snowflake in no time. Snowflake was available on demand, meaning no contract was required, no need to own or manage hardware, and no upfront investments. All a new customer needed was a network connection to access the public cloud. At first, Snowflake ran on Amazon Web Services. Later, it branched out to run on Microsoft's and Google's versions of the public cloud. With Snowflake, customers pay only for what they use in machine seconds, a highly granular and elastic model.

To top things off, the Snowflake founders designed the platform to be self-managing and self-provisioning. Database administrators, the druids of data management, need not apply. Snowflake did away with the DBA. This was one powerful cocktail of scale, performance, economy, usability, and simplicity.

Benoit, Thierry, and Mike (Marcin came later) saw an opportunity to combine the capabilities of existing databases, including traditional relational databases, which organize conventional enterprise data in columns and rows. They redesigned the technology to handle huge amounts of diverse data types and moved all that goodness to the cloud. They created the first data warehouse built from the ground up to fully exploit the tremendous scale and performance of cloud computing.

In the process, they pioneered a new class of cloud computing, the Data Cloud. Other cloud categories include the infrastructure and storage clouds, which obviate the need for enterprises to buy and manage their own computers and storage devices, and Software-as-a-Service applications running in the cloud, which relieve enterprises of the burden of purchasing and managing complex software applications. The Data Cloud holds and manages an enterprise's data, which these days is being recognized as an incredibly valuable asset.

This approach makes all kinds of data available to anybody with permission to use it via a simple and inexpensive mechanism, Snowflake's cloud data warehouse. And the technology assures that there is only one version of any data collection—one version of the truth. Over the years, Snowflake's technology vision has expanded to become what we call the cloud data platform (CDP), which adds a number of important capabilities to the core data warehouse technology as well as tight integration with third-party technology and data providers.

This technology helps to fulfill a dream the business and tech communities have long hoped for: running a full-on digital enterprise. At last, practically every move a company makes can be driven by data and governed by software. People can understand more deeply than ever before what has already happened, and they can predict with authority what is likely to happen next. At the same time, the platform democratizes access to superior insights mined from data. Anybody with a credit card can tap into some of the most sophisticated data analytics technologies on the planet, including artificial intelligence.

Because of this new design, people at Snowflake don't talk about Big Data anymore. It's just data. We don't care if it's big, small, or somewhere in between. The technology architecture that the founders invented handles it all. Without breaking a sweat. As a result, every enterprise—every business—can be like Google or Facebook in terms of how they mobilize data.

Snowflake is as of this writing processing 400 million queries a day. And that number continues to grow at nearly 200 percent annually. You can see why I jumped at the chance to lead the company.

WHERE I CAME FROM

This wasn't my first rodeo. I had the pleasure and honor of leading two remarkable tech companies before Snowflake.

The first was Data Domain, which was started in 2001 by Kai Li, Ben Zhu, and Brian Biles. They were pioneers in replacing electromagnetic tape data storage with disk storage. Tape was cheap, but the equipment occupied a lot of space and was error-prone. It also took too much time to access data. The Data Domain founders invented a new class of data center storage that eliminated redundant data before it was written to disk, reducing volume by 95 percent. That made it economical to store more data on disk, where it could be quickly accessed. Their invention had the potential to turn a multibillion-dollar market upside down.

When I joined as CEO eighteen months after Data Domain was started, the company had just twenty employees, no customers, no revenue, and was almost out of money. We raised capital, put the nascent business on track, grew revenue rapidly, and took the company public in 2007. After a high-profile bidding war between NetApp and EMC in the summer of 2009, EMC bought Data Domain for $2.4 billion in cash and stock. Data Domain became the cornerstone of EMC's newly formed Backup Recovery Systems Division, which I ran for two years. Data Domain is a formidable business to this day in the larger Dell/EMC family of technologies.

Next came ServiceNow. Fred Luddy started the company in 2003 with the goal of building a self-service cloud application to enable businesses to automate routine IT operations and projects. Not long after I joined as CEO in 2011, we took the company public with a valuation of more than $2 billion. We expanded to provide self-service for other business processes, including HR, customer service, facilities, security, and field service. Revenue grew from $100 million the year I joined to $1.4 billion in 2016. At that time, it was the fastest-growing enterprise cloud software company in the world. Today, its market cap is upwards of $64 billion.

By 2017, though, I was done. I had been in the line of fire for so long, and I wasn't enjoying it anymore. I didn't realize it at the time, but I was burned out. Not something a vacation can fix.

So I found my successor and I moved on.

For a time, I settled comfortably into retirement in Pleasanton. We raced my TP52, a grand prix yacht named *Invisible Hand*, all over the Western Hemisphere. We won many races, including the 2017 Transpac Overall—2,225 nautical miles from California to Hawaii. Because there is a limit to how much you can sail, I created a personal investment vehicle I called Invisible Hand Ventures. I invested in a handful of startups per year alongside VC friends, and I made myself available to the CEOs of the companies I invested in if they wanted somebody to bounce ideas off of. I never expected to lead another company. I was out.

Then Mike emailed me.

In a flash, the fires were reignited. I was ready to go, inspired, batteries charged. Yes, I had told myself over and over that I was done. But there's a problem. People like me, we're not made to sit on the sidelines. We crave the arena, the action and excitement. We love to lead and help a company grow. Who knows, maybe we're also spoiling for another brawl.

I spent the next few days with members of Snowflake's board at the offices of Mike's VC firm, Sutter Hill Ventures. The marathon meetings included Benoit and Thierry, some of the venture capitalists who backed the company, and some seasoned enterprise software executives who serve on the board.

The most compelling factor for me was Snowflake's technology architecture—the first data platform designed from scratch to run at cloud scale. The computer scientists behind it were extremely talented. Technical co-founders Benoit, Thierry, and Marcin had more than 120 patents to their names. I suspected that this company had the potential to disrupt the $45 billion enterprise database market. Someday, it might even vie for the position Oracle occupied as the leader in data management software. But this time, in the cloud.

That settled it. I had had more than two years of rest, and I was ready to go. I wanted to take the field again. The board wanted me. The deal was done.

When I showed up for duty at Snowflake's offices last April, I faced a group of people who had varying degrees of concern about what my arrival would mean. The company had come a long way in the five years since it came out of stealth mode in 2014. Back then, it was an unknown quantity with a funny name. By the time I joined, Snowflake had been growing rapidly and hiring rapidly for years. It was known in the marketplace and had scored a coveted "Leader" designation in Gartner's Magic Quadrant for the data management industry. It ranked right up there with Oracle, Microsoft, and Amazon. Nobody was laughing at the name Snowflake anymore.

For this remarkable rise, credit goes to our incredible founders, and to Mike Speiser and Bob Muglia. Bob brought passion for products and people to Snowflake. He charted a path where few companies had gone before. While Benoit, Thierry, and Marcin were the keepers of the technology vision, Bob helped out with product management. He left his mark on everything from pricing strategies to partnerships to sales. He also spearheaded the capitalization of the company with Mike. The hundreds of millions he raised enabled the company to hire the engineers it needed to rapidly add features to the product and to build a global sales force.

My job was to maintain the blistering growth trajectory, but this time at scale. I had to continue to expand on the company's technology leadership while improving business processes—the efficiency and effectiveness of the organization. I had to rapidly scale what the team had incubated. I brought with me some key members of my leadership teams at ServiceNow and at Data Domain, including Mike Scarpelli as CFO and Shelly Begun as head of HR. We shifted some leadership roles and hired new talent—and, yes, we asked some people to leave. We put Benoit back in charge of products, where in my view he should have been all along. We examined everything the company did and why it did it. We found ways to optimize spending and streamline operations. We turned over every rock until there were none left.

I am certain all this rapid-fire action added stress to the lives of many Snowflake employees. A leadership change inevitably does. My personality probably added to the stress. I am high-intensity, impatient, and engaged. I am also profoundly malcontented, never satisfied with the status quo, always seeing the variance between what is and what could be. No high-fiving, self-congratulation, or victory laps for me. That is a departure from the feel-good culture in Silicon Valley. I do not wait around for problems to manifest themselves, so stepping up the pace is part of our regimen.

After I came on as CEO, nearly every reporter asked me the same question: When will Snowflake go public? The short answer was that I wasn't hired just to take the company out, though I have done that twice before as CEO and many more times as a board director. IPOs are a step along the way. They come and they go. The work is still there the next day. The novelty of an IPO has long worn off for me and my core team, but we understood that it is a huge deal for Snowflake employees and other stakeholders. We didn't have a specific timeline for going public other than that we were in the middle of preparing ourselves to be able to do it when we felt like pulling that trigger. My job is to scale the company, as a private and as a public company.

THE ESSENCE OF SNOWFLAKE: TECHNOLOGY

Let's get back to the essence of Snowflake: its technology. Snowflake was built as a broadly capable cloud data platform but with an initial focus on a specific workload: the analytical data processing associated with a data warehouse. The reasons are straightforward. Analytical processing and data warehousing have suffered from scale and performance limitations ever since the terms came into vogue. Truly built from the ground up for cloud computing, Snowflake could raise the roof on scale and performance simultaneously. The market would beat a path to our door to get its hands on this breakthrough. And it did.

A data warehouse is essentially a digital container where all kinds of data can be managed, organized, integrated, and queried. The beauty of moving data warehousing to the cloud is that there are no limits on data volume and computing capacity. You have unlimited storage and computing resources at your fingertips.

Our technology founders made the groundbreaking move of separating storage from computing. As a result, our customers pay very little to store their data in the cloud, and they pay for computing resources only as they use them. This makes it a no-brainer for organizations to move their data to the cloud.

The second major element of our cloud architecture is performance. Traditionally, high-end data analytics was performed in the data center by directing a number of tasks at a single cluster of computers. At busy times, that created a data traffic jam that looked like the parking lot at Walmart on a Saturday afternoon.

Snowflake's founders designed our system so individual computing tasks are pointed at a single cluster of computers dedicated to each task (or several clusters). Nothing gets in their way and slows them down. Meanwhile, the founders created what they called a multi-cluster shared-storage architecture, meaning that all computing clusters tap into a single data store. Within a large organization, each department or group can have its own dedicated clusters, but they are all using the same pool of data.

In the past, our industry and its customers had been constrained by data volume and computing capacity. Now, thanks to the cloud, we can apply unlimited computing resources to unlimited amounts of data. As a result of the design decisions made by our founders, computing jobs that typically required hours or days to handle on traditional systems can be completed in minutes or even seconds.

The third major element of our cloud data warehouse is its ease of use. Our customers operate totally within our cloud environment. They don't have to see or interact with or get billed by the public cloud provider. We handle all that for them. Further, the system was designed to be self-managed and self-provisioning. Large customers don't have to assign armies of database black belts to manage it. Small customers—even individuals who run their own businesses—can get going in a few minutes. Small businesses don't have to sign a contract. We monitor their usage to the machine second so they only get billed for what they use.

This is a key point. In the old days of enterprise computing, companies typically paid millions of dollars to license a package of software, millions more to buy the hardware and to get the software installed properly, and then more money for yearly maintenance contracts. Think Oracle. Then came Software-as-a-Service, or SaaS. The customer negotiated a price with the software supplier and paid monthly to use software that ran in the cloud. Think Salesforce. Now, we have the utilization model, with payments based on consumption. You buy credits and use them when you need them. Think Amazon's AWS and Snowflake. We believe it's a superior model and that someday most enterprise software will be purchased and delivered this way.

A key feature of the Snowflake technology that I want to touch on is data sharing. In business and government, the sharing of data within an organization and between organizations has always been difficult. Because of Snowflake's cloud architecture, though, select pieces of data can easily be shared on a one-to-one basis or one to many. This is done without making or moving copies of data, which could lead to discrepancies as well as governance violations.

The data warehouse is the beating heart of our cloud data platform. The founders had the platform firmly in mind when they started the company, but the first step was the data warehouse. For the past couple of years, they've been filling out the platform vision and technology.

People should think of a cloud data platform as the entire supply chain of data—from where it originates to where it is kept to where it is fully analyzed and acted on. As important, the platform supports a wide range of use cases and workloads.

We call it a platform for several reasons. In the broadest sense, it's a foundation upon which companies large and small can build their strategies and methods for managing data and getting more value from it.

It's also a platform like a computer operating system, in some ways. Our CDP enables independent software companies to build applications on top of it. Also, as with a computer operating system, third parties provide tools, computer programming languages, and utilities that help companies get the most out of our platform.

An essential piece of our platform is the data exchange. We take the basic sharing capability I talked about earlier and add features that turn it into a marketplace for data. It's many-to-many data sharing.

If data analytics software was an automobile, our cloud data platform would be the chassis.

HOW SNOWFLAKE HELPS BUSINESSES BECOME DATA DRIVEN

Our cloud data platform addresses the needs of a wide variety of businesses, government agencies, and nonprofit organizations.

For born-in-the-cloud startups, the Snowflake platform enables them to get up and running quickly with minimal costs, and to pay as they go. Many of these companies do everything in the cloud, from managing internal processes to selling to interacting with customers. The platform allows every functional and geographical group within a company to access all of the company's data at the same time and rest assured that they're all using the same facts and numbers. It makes the organization nimble and the people in it informed, up to date, and aligned with one another.

Take the case of Fair. The company is disrupting automotive leasing and financing by giving its customers the unprecedented ability to shop, get approved, and sign to lease a pre-owned car entirely on their phones. There is no long-term commitment, negotiation, or physical paperwork. To apply, customers enter their email and phone number via the Fair smartphone app. If approved, they can shop by brand, model, or dealer. They see only cars with monthly payments they can afford. Customers can sign into the Fair app with a finger, set up a payment method, pay the upfront costs, pick up the vehicle, and drive off. They can drive the vehicle for as long they want, paying monthly as they go. When they're done, they simply turn the car in with at least five days' notice.

In 2017, shortly after launching the company, Fair's leaders realized they needed a data management system that enabled their people to access a wide range of data and make decisions in real time. Initially, they had about 50 traditional relational databases handling an array of data, including information from their Salesforce customer relationship management system and their NetSuite financial applications. Managing the system was labor-intensive, and it was difficult to combine data from the different databases.

After Fair shifted to Snowflake, it established one version of the truth that everybody could tap into. Today, the company is piping in more than 40 million data records per day and running 50 to 100 queries simultaneously. This enables them to do things like adjust and optimize pricing on the fly. It also slashes management overhead. "Our Snowflake expense for the entire year is less than the costs of one data engineer," says Brandon Adams, director for analytics at Fair.

On the other end of the spectrum, we're helping large established companies move their data ecosystems to the cloud. We find that while many such companies were initially wary of moving the lion's share of their computing tasks to the cloud, they have changed their minds and are now rapidly migrating to the cloud. They understand that the cloud model solves their scaling challenges and reduces IT capital expenditures dramatically, even as it makes their data more secure.

Take Capital One, a banking giant and an exemplar of technology innovation. Capital One was among the first in the industry to embrace the cloud. Now it's all in.

"The business imperative is to be able to give personalized unique experiences to each of our customers," says Linda Apsley, the bank's former vice president for data engineering. She has since left the company.

Capital One believed in the value of Snowflake's technology and made an investment through Capital One Growth Ventures, the company's VC arm, in 2017.

A third major category of Snowflake customers comprises the hundreds of companies that build software products on top of Snowflake for analyzing data—which they then sell to their customers. Think of the Snowflake data platform as a huge lake. These companies are like the organizations that draw water from a lake for drinking, to put out fires, to irrigate farm fields, or to cool nuclear reactors. They are Snowflake's customers *and* partners.

One example is Blackboard, the largest education technology and services company in the world. It has 16,000 schools as customers in 90 countries and serves more than 100 million students. Its products include teaching and learning platforms, applications for managing schools and serving students, and analytics products for improving the performance of organizations and individual learners.

Blackboard adopted Snowflake more than three years ago as its company-wide cloud data warehouse. Today, all of the data it collects for many of its customers resides in Snowflake. It's one of the largest educational datasets in the world. Blackboard is now enabling its customers to share data with other customers and organizations that sell products and services to them. "We're trying to create a data and analytics platform in the education space that helps our customers better leverage and share their data," says Jay White, Blackboard's vice president for software engineering.

Jay's engineering group develops analytics-based products that schools use to improve their effectiveness. One such product is for student advisers. It ingests a wide variety of data about individual students, including biographical info, demographics, and grades from past courses taken. Using predictive analytics, it identifies students at risk. With this information, the advisers can devote their time to those who are likely to benefit most from an intervention. Jay's team wrote the application and integrated it with Snowflake's data warehouse in just six months. That was a record time for that kind of a project.

DATA NETWORK EFFECTS

I don't want to get too carried away with technology in this introduction. You'll learn more about it in later chapters. But I do want to spend a minute talking about the value of data sharing. Back in the mid-1990s, with the emergence of the Internet, computer industry leaders and economists began talking excitedly about a concept, network effects, that they used to describe the value that was created by connecting millions of people via the Net. The term was actually coined in the early days of the twentieth century when AT&T, then called Bell Telephone, began buying local carriers to create what eventually became a national telephone monopoly.

The concept took on new currency and power once observers noted that the more people you get to connect to the Internet and to websites, the more value the network creates for the individuals and for the businesses that interact with them there. The ultimate expression of the value of network effects on the Internet are Facebook and Google, where their ability to present advertising to billions of people has created a combined total market capitalization topping $1.5 trillion.

But Facebook and Google didn't rack up those huge valuations based solely on their ability to create ad impressions upon a huge number of people. Thanks to the vast amount of data they collect about habits and tastes of their users, they are able to target ads more precisely than other Internet companies. In this case, precision translates into money. Think of this added value they create as *data* network effects.

Here's how I define data network effects: The more organizations make their data available to others, and the more data that exists in that pool, the more value accrues to all of the organizations that participate in the data-sharing network. This in turn attracts more participants to the network.

Very few companies have access to the amount of actionable data that Facebook and Google do. (Maybe only Amazon comes close.) But that doesn't mean that others can't reap tremendous value from data network effects.

In some cases, such as with banks, organizations already have a tremendous amount of information about their customers and their internal operations. Unfortunately, much of the information is stored in isolated databases that are controlled by the business units that gather those specific chunks of data—and which prevent their colleagues in other business units from accessing it.

This is what the industry refers to as data silos.

Other types of businesses lack access to critical data that could help them better understand their customers, distribution channels, and suppliers. Sure, there is some sharing going on between large organizations and their business partners, but it's often a one-way street—with most of the value flowing to the behemoth at the center of the web of commercial activity. The others are data-deprived.

Again, data flow is inhibited.

At Snowflake, we think the key to unleashing the value of data network effects is the massive, promiscuous, and frequent sharing of all types of data. This includes sharing among units within a company and among business partners. It includes sales of data by those who create or gather it to those who need it, subject to data policies and governance rules. If data is to fulfill its tremendous potential for transforming business and fueling the economy, it must be liberated from the restraints of legacy computing and legacy thinking.

We facilitate sharing with our technology, both in the data warehouses and in the new public and private exchanges. We provide direct and secure data sharing within seconds so enterprises can easily forge one-to-one, one-to-many, and many-to-many relationships.

If Facebook is the ultimate expression of *social* sharing for individuals, we aim to be the ultimate expression of *data* sharing for enterprises.

HOW WE COMPETE

Snowflake competes with some of the most powerful companies in the tech universe. We also collaborate with them. And we are their customers. It's a novel set of relationship dynamics that we are still settling into. As I mentioned earlier, Snowflake is available as a service running on the three major public clouds: AWS, Microsoft's Azure, and Google's cloud.

We're a large customer because we run Snowflake deployments on these clouds. We're also a partner because we collaborate with them to migrate on-premise workloads to the cloud and to improve the interoperability of our technologies. But we're a competitor to all three because they have their own data warehouses running on their clouds.

The Big Three can easily see how much of our customers' data we have in their storage and how many computing jobs we're running for them, so they know just how fast we're growing. That may be unsettling.

Because these three companies control the vast majority of public cloud computing, they get the first shot at potential data warehousing customers. This means we have to offer a substantially superior product. We achieve this in a number of ways. Our platform is highly differentiated in terms of its capabilities, but another selling point is this: As far as I know, we are the only cloud data warehouse that runs on all three public clouds. We find that some enterprises want to spread their computing across more than one public cloud so they don't become locked into a single vendor. Because we run everywhere and those cloud giants don't, our value proposition is attractive to customers who want to avoid lock-in.

The term "co-opetition" was coined in the 1990s by networking software pioneer Ray Noorda to describe a phenomenon he saw unfolding in the PC software business. It was the idea that software companies that competed with each other also needed to cooperate—for their own benefit and for the good of their customers. This describes our relationships with Amazon, Microsoft, and Google. A more recent term is "frenemies."

Truth be told, things can get testy at times. But it's a huge market, and we figure out how to control the fighting impulses so that together we perform for the customers we serve.

Competition is good. It makes us better. Steel sharpens steel. We cannot rest on our laurels as one of the fastest-growing enterprise cloud companies. We know that if we become complacent, we will surely have our heads handed to us—if not by Amazon, Microsoft, or Google, then by new entrants whose names are not even known to us yet.

Still, we take pleasure in challenging them on their own platforms. The way we see things, Snowflake layers across these three islands of infrastructure. We have key competitive advantages. At my previous companies, I used to periodically tell my boards of directors what kept me up at night. But these days I answer that question differently: I now sleep like a baby, and I keep others up at night.

Consider these factoids: Google processes about 6 billion searches per day. Snowflake today handles an average of more than 400 million data queries per day, and the popularity of our service is exploding. What Google is for Web pages, Snowflake is trending to be for data.

DATA UNLEASHED

What I think about after I turn the lights out is the huge wave that we're riding—the Data Cloud. I've been in the tech industry for more than 25 years. I've worked for a bunch of companies, including Compuware, Borland, EMC, and of course Data Domain and ServiceNow. I've seen many waves of innovation rise and crest. But I've never participated in a wave as big as this—with so much potential to reshape business, society, and the lives of individuals.

Sometimes it takes longer than you would expect for the big wave to develop. I think initial wariness on the part of the large enterprises toward the public cloud slowed things a bit. But now enterprises large and small are ready to go. Technology and business leaders have run out of excuses.

My advice to CEOs and CIOs and others who make strategic decisions is to be aggressive adopters of these new data technologies. I'm not talking about living on the bleeding edge, but organizations must have the will and the muscle to transition steadily from one technology platform to the next. Some leaders are afraid of risk, yet it is the job of the CEO to manage risk. Understanding technology and managing technology—these are critical attributes for literally every organization. That's because, in a sense, they're all becoming technology companies.

We are in the middle of a great migration of technology and information and commerce to the cloud. First it was websites and search engines and e-commerce stores. Then came cloud computing infrastructure services, Software-as-a-Service applications, and smartphone apps.

The Data Cloud is the latest phase of that great migration. Much of the existing data in the world is moving to the cloud, and at the same time there is an explosion of new sources and types of data. In the cloud, data is secure, accessible, combinable, shareable, and analyzable. Thanks to all this data in the cloud, we are able to understand how businesses work and how humans operate—what they want and how they want it—with much more precision and certainty than ever before. And we can get those insights in seconds.

Take time to let that fully sink in. It's not some secondary thing. In many cases, data is the most important asset that a company possesses, often without realizing it, so CEOs should not hand the data leadership role to somebody else. The vision and the mandate must come from the top.

* * *

This book is about the power of the Data Cloud—told through Snow-flake, its customers, and its partners. We're publishing it at a time of great uncertainty, when the world is in the throes of the coronavirus crisis. Nobody knows for sure what will happen next, but, over the long haul, we're confident business and society will regain their stability and vitality. It seems likely that data and the Data Cloud will play major roles in the global economic recovery.

I wrote this introduction to give you my point of view on the company, the technology, and the industry. We hired freelance writer Steve Hamm, a veteran tech journalist and author, to help us tell our story. He spoke extensively to me, members of my executive team, and dozens of people from Snowflake, our customers, and our partners. He takes over from here. I'll come back at the end to sum up and look into the future.

The book is aimed at business leaders who are bold enough to harness cutting-edge technologies to address problems, exploit opportunities, or literally transform their businesses. It's for entrepreneurs who want to help build the data economy. And it's for investors who are willing to place exciting bets and grow with America in the twenty-first century. I hope you find it useful and inspiring.

PART 1

SNOWFLAKE

An Emerging Player
in the Data Economy

1

THE BIG IDEA

T'S AMAZING how you can begin something with an idea that turns out to be a non-starter but end up in an incredibly promising place anyway. That's what happened in the early days of Snowflake.

The seeds for the company were developed and planted by Mike Speiser, a managing director at the venture capital firm Sutter Hill Ventures. Back in 2010, he started thinking about the next enterprise technology startup he could help launch.

Sutter Hill Ventures has an unusual business model. The more typical VC strategy is to search for promising startups that have already been formed and invest in them. Sutter Hill's partners do some of that, but they also analyze the tech landscape and try to spot nascent companies that they can incubate within their own offices. They even do initial engineering and design prototyping in-house. Once they've agreed to form a company in a promising area, they recruit technical founders with deep expertise. Then, off they go.

Before Snowflake, Mike was the founding investor for Pure Storage and served as CEO for a little more than one year. The company was a pioneer in replacing disk storage devices in enterprise data centers with faster, more reliable, and more compact solid-state storage devices—so-called flash storage. They based their storage architecture on flash memory chips instead of the traditional mechanical disk.

Even before Mike gave up the CEO role at Pure Storage, he had begun thinking about what he would do next. Because of his vantage point there, he was one of the few people in the world who understood the impact that flash storage could have on the enterprise data center. Computers would be able to access data 100 times faster than before. But traditional databases had been designed to run with disk storage, so he figured there was a huge opportunity to design a database optimized to run on flash.

Mike thinks of himself as being an entrepreneur within a venture capital firm. He's a founding investor and board member at no fewer than ten tech startups, including Observe, Sigma Computing, and Clumio. Earlier in his career he was a co-founder of Epinions.com, the pioneering consumer review website, worked for Symantec, and joined Yahoo through the acquisition of another company he co-founded.

When he's investigating a new business idea, his approach is to talk to a lot of smart people and see what they think of it. "Bayesian learning is at the core of all machine learning, and I'm a human Bayesian," he says. "I develop an idea, and then I go and talk to a lot of people and make my idea better and better. Or, if it turns out to be a bad idea, I drop it."

Over a period of nearly two years, Sutter Hill's engineering recruiting partner, Doug Mohr, introduced Mike to dozens of computer science professors and software architects who were experts in the storage and database fields. Some of them showed interest in his flash database pitch; others did not. None of them gave him a satisfyingly clear explanation for their conclusions.

Finally, Doug introduced Mike to Benoit Dageville, a native of France who was then one of the top software architects at Oracle, the largest database software company in the world. This was in early 2012. Benoit visited Sutter Hill's offices in Palo Alto, Calif., listened to Mike's pitch, and gave him some surprising feedback.

He called the idea "cute."

Mike had lived in France for a summer when he was in college. He had heard the word "cute" used in this way by French people before. It meant "not good," but in a nice sort of way.

Mike doesn't get hung up on being right. He just wants to arrive at the right answer ultimately. So he wasn't offended. He pressed Benoit for an explanation. They spoke for hours at the office and picked up the conversation later over a couple of dinners.

Benoit told him, "You're solving a problem that isn't a problem."

A BETTER IDEA

Benoit talked about how all database systems have two components—storage and computation. The key element of the storage component is the ability of the system to read and write data quickly. This is called Input/Output, or I/O. The computational part is about being able to take lots of disparate pieces of information and process them quickly—turning data into insights.

True, designing databases so they would have faster I/O, as Mike suggested, would be a good thing. There was value in creating a storage-driven approach to making the database perform better. But, Benoit told him, if you wanted to do something really dramatic—what would be a huge boon to businesses—you would focus on the computational side.

At Oracle, Benoit spent a lot of time talking to customers about their computing needs and their frustrations. Two things they complained about frequently were the cost and complexity of computing. As the amount of data they handled exploded, and as additional types of data were added to the mix, they had to purchase more powerful—and more expensive—computers and software to deal with it.

A company called Teradata had made a mint selling computers and software that crunched data the expensive way. Teradata popularized one of the more important software concepts in the history of computing—the data warehouse, where data of all types could be more effectively collected, managed, and accessed for analysis.

But Oracle customers had told Benoit that they wished there were better and cheaper ways to process data. That, Benoit said, is where Mike should focus. A startup with brilliant technology might be able to double I/O performance in the database, but it might not be able to improve computational performance by a hundredfold.

At the time, cloud computing was taking off. Amazon.com's public cloud offered businesses the opportunity to offload the headaches of purchasing and managing computers and storage devices and of running their own data centers. Instead, customers paid Amazon and other cloud operators to handle these tasks. One of the advantages of cloud computing is that customers aren't constrained by the computer resources they own. Their ability to get computing jobs done on demand is practically limitless.

Mike and Benoit didn't arrive at Snowflake's core concept in a rush. There was no magical "aha!" moment. But, gradually, an idea crystalized: They would create a data warehouse in the cloud that had the potential to massively exceed what Teradata had done in on-premises data centers. They would offer customers a more effective and less expensive method for handling large amounts of diverse data—and there would be zero limits on storage or computing resources.

WHERE OUR FOUNDERS CAME FROM

Benoit was one of the leading experts at designing software to enable powerful clusters of computers to process data rapidly and efficiently. His specialty was parallelization. That's a type of computation where many calculations are carried out simultaneously. Large problems are divided into smaller pieces and farmed out to different microprocessors, then the results are combined. It gets computing tasks done quickly and makes efficient use of computing resources.

He grew up in France. As a teenager, he wasn't interested in computers at first. He owned a motorcycle and loved to ride it and tinker with it. But then a classmate brought a programmable calculator to school one day and showed him how to program it. The calculator asked Benoit for his name. He typed it in. It shot back: "Benoit, you are an ass!" He loved it. He was amazed that you could have a conversation (of sorts) with a computer. He became obsessed with programming. He later created a computer game, which he sold to a French company.

At Pierre and Marie Curie University in Paris. Benoit studied computer science and ultimately got a PhD in the field. His thesis focused on running the SQL data query language on parallel systems, processing massive amounts of data. Right out of university he got what he saw as a chance of a lifetime—to work on a pan-European research project, the European Strategic Program on Research in Information Technology. But in time he learned that he didn't like research so much. He would rather build powerful computing systems than write papers about computer science. So he went to work for Bull Information Systems, which, in the 1980s, was a significant player in Europe's computer industry

The center of gravity for the tech world was far away, in Silicon Valley, and Benoit longed to be in the middle of the action. He got a shot when Bull sent him there in the mid-1990s to work on a project with Oracle. After a few months, he went to work *for* Oracle.

It was a great place for Benoit. He got to work on some of the biggest challenges in data management and data processing. He soon was promoted to the role of architect, which, in the tech world, is a bit like being the wizard Merlin in the Court of King Arthur. You are frequently called upon by colleagues and customers to perform technology magic. Few people really understand what you do, but they respect you for it.

Yet as comfortable and stimulating as Oracle was for Benoit, he occasionally felt the tug of adventures beyond the company's walls. In the late 1990s, during the dot-com era, he was briefly lured away to a high-flying Internet grocery delivery service called Webvan. He was one of many of Oracle's talented computer scientists and engineers who were recruited to the dot-coms—many of which eventually went bust. After his fling with Webvan, Benoit returned to Oracle.

It was in the late 1990s that Benoit and Thierry Cruanes became colleagues and friends. Thierry got his PhD at the same university and in the same program as Benoit. He had grown up in a small farming town in the north of France. His first encounter with a computer came at about age 12 at an agricultural fair, among the tractors, cattle, and sheep. It was an Apple Lisa, the one that came before Macintosh. But, once he saw it work, he was captivated by the idea that computer scientists could build machines that could mimic the human brain. That was magical. Like Benoit before him, Thierry started writing simple programs for a calculator and progressed from there.

Throughout Thierry's career, he found one magical technology after another to learn about and master. He loved the database field because, "When you open a database, as an engineer, you find all of the computer science field in it. It's computer science in a box," Thierry says.

Benoit recalls that he and Thierry first spoke on the phone. It was a long-distance call between France and Silicon Valley. Colleagues at Oracle had approached Benoit. They planned on interviewing a job candidate from France whose accent was too thick for them to understand.

That was Thierry. They pressed Benoit into service to do the first interview. After Oracle hired Thierry, the two became close friends.

A decade later, Benoit was ready to leave Oracle—and he wanted Thierry to go with him. Benoit had been there for sixteen years, and, despite his professional satisfaction, he was frustrated that Oracle was slow to embrace cloud computing. Also, the company was seemingly incapable of scaling its systems to respond to the Big Data revolution—the explosion in the quantity and variety of data that was sweeping the worlds of technology and business.

Oracle's database division at the time was releasing a major upgrade of its software for on-premises computing about every four years. With cloud computing, software could be improved continuously. When Benoit started working at Oracle, engineers would spend about 60 percent of their time developing new products and features, and the rest of the time fixing bugs on existing products. In his last year, engineering was spending 90 percent of its time on bug fixes. That was incredibly frustrating.

Benoit felt that Oracle had become a dinosaur, and he was becoming a little dinosaur inside Oracle. He told Thierry: "We have to leave. We have to do something. We are dying here."

Thierry recalls the difficulty he was having hiring people for his product engineering team. At that time, he was a manager and Benoit was an architect. The brightest young computer scientists fresh out of university didn't want to work for Oracle. They wanted to be part of the Big Data revolution.

THE DREAM OF CREATING A NEW DATABASE

Thierry and Benoit began to meet at lunchtime at a table outside Building 400 at Oracle's headquarters campus in Redwood City, California. It was just off the San Francisco Bay, and typically there was a pleasant breeze. Benoit drank one cup of coffee after another. They discussed the trends that were sweeping the tech industry—and seemingly leaving them behind. They saw how excited many in the industry were about Hadoop, the open source technology that many in the tech industry were using to manage the explosion of data, but they also saw the limitations of Hadoop. It was too complicated.

Meanwhile, they both started looking for jobs at other tech companies. They had no thought of launching a startup themselves at that point. Yet, amazingly, the first call Benoit got was from Doug Mohr, Mike Speiser's headhunter colleague. He was calling about a chief technologist job at one of Sutter Hill's portfolio companies. That one wasn't a good fit, but a week later, Doug called back and said Mike wanted to talk about something else: the flash database.

A few weeks later, after Benoit and Mike decided that they should focus on building a really big data warehouse in the cloud, Benoit talked to Thierry again. "I told him, there is this crazy guy. He thinks we can build a new database and it would be as big as Oracle."

This was a tremendously exciting time. After all those years of seeing Oracle customers suffer because of the complexity of the software, Benoit relished the idea of giving them a computing service that they wouldn't have to tinker with. And, as a software development guy, he looked forward to being able to constantly improve the software rather than updating it every few years. He also liked the idea of developing a database that could handle all kinds of information, not just the traditional data organized in columns and rows. By starting from a blank page, he and Thierry could build a new kind of database designed for modern computing. "It was a dream database," he says. "We had the idea on what to do, but we had no clue how to do it."

Mike was sizing up the business opportunity. The worldwide database market at the time was about $45 billion. The data warehouse piece by itself was over $10 billion. That segment of the market was growing much faster than the largest part, the relational database, because of the rise of

Big Data and the emergence of artificial intelligence tools with which to perform analysis. So it was a plenty big target for a small company.

Mike believed that these two French guys, accents and all, had the potential to do something that had never been done before. "That takes real vision. A real vision comes from somebody who is an artist. I thought these guys were artists," he says. Also, he liked them because they were not arrogant—unlike a lot of other startup founders he had met. Benoit and Thierry didn't think they were right about everything. They were earnestly searching for the right answers.

SNOWFLAKE IS BORN

At last, they decided to form a company. Mike was to be the interim CEO, and Benoit and Thierry would be the co-founders and chief technologists. Sutter Hill invested $1 million to get things started. Looking back from today, Snowflake's executives believe that one of the keys to the company's success so far is that Benoit and Thierry did not insist on being the business leaders of the company, unlike so many other founders of Silicon Valley startups. That enabled people with business expertise to lead while Benoit and Thierry focused on what they did best, innovation.

In early August of 2012, Benoit and Thierry resigned from Oracle and set up offices in a small apartment Benoit rented in downtown San Mateo. Their first purchase was a large whiteboard. Then they bought computers. Thierry liked Apple's Macs. Benoit didn't. Thierry won that argument. They mounted the whiteboard on a wall in the living room. "We looked at it and said, O.K., now we have to redesign for the cloud," Benoit says.

They spent weeks talking and writing on the whiteboard. They began by listing the issues that corporations faced. These were the problems they wanted their database to solve. It would be in the cloud so there would be no restraints on capacity and it could run really fast. It had to be able to handle all types of data. It had to be self-service and really simple to use. Business units in a company should not have to ask the IT department to set up the system for them.

Initially, they thought they would build their own cloud rather than running the database on one of the existing public clouds. They sketched out a variety of hardware configurations, including, potentially, using flash storage. Later, they realized that they could get the hardware performance they needed from the big cloud vendors.

Benoit and Thierry were steeped in the knowledge of how to make traditional databases running in conventional data centers. But with this project, they had to rethink and reinvent the database—and how the software interacted with the hardware. "We almost had to forget what we knew," Thierry says.

For the first six months, it was basically two guys in a room working really long hours. Thierry did the cooking. Benoit drank endless cups of coffee.

In those early months, they made two important architectural decisions.

The first was to separate storage from computing. A company would maintain just one copy of all of the data it collected. The data would be placed in the cloud. The data warehouse would map that data and draw records from databases in it as needed. Any number of clusters of computers would be directed to access the same data at the same time.

This architecture had two primary advantages. It meant there was only one version of the truth within a company—not a mishmash of databases that might have outdated or incorrect information in them. Also, it meant that they could store a customer's data on an array of storage devices within a public cloud and charge the customer for storage separately from computing. They would charge mainly for data in motion. Stored data would be highly compressed and very inexpensive.

That encouraged customers to move all of their data to the cloud and to Snowflake's data warehouse.

The second critical design decision they made was to change the way they used computing resources. In conventional scenarios, many software applications and database queries tap into a cluster of computers. It's done that way so all of the users can access computing power concurrently. Nobody has to wait to get started. But the problem comes when too many users are online at the same time. The system slows to a crawl.

Thanks to the cloud, organizations can have access to practically unlimited computing resources. The cloud is "elastic," making it possible to assign a big computing job exclusively to an entire cluster of computers or even more than one cluster. No resource sharing is required. By designing for the cloud, Benoit and Thierry made a database management system that processes queries in seconds rather than minutes or days.

Startup founders have to pick a name for their company early on—sometimes before they're completely sure what they will ultimately make and sell. They know that whatever they choose will probably stick until they sell the company to somebody else or fail. So naming is ultra-important. These guys didn't want a run-of-the-mill name. They wanted something that popped. Mike suggested Snowflake because he, Benoit, and Thierry all enjoyed skiing and being in the mountains. Also, snow comes from the clouds. So Snowflake it would be.

One of their first hires was Marcin Zukowski. He was running a tech company, Vectorwise, which he had started in the Netherlands after he got his PhD from a university there. Its technology was based on work he had done in grad school—a method for improving the performance of databases called vectorized query execution.

Traditionally, databases respond to queries by fetching a single record at a time. With vectorized execution, the system fetches a large number of records in each processing cycle, rather than just one. Think of it this way: You're a student buying beer for a party. In the liquor store, you don't select one beer at a time from a case and bring it to the cash register; you bring the whole case. As the quantities of data to be analyzed soared, the tech world needed more efficient ways of accessing it. This was one of them.

"We knew we needed this technology and we needed Marcin," says Benoit. "We also knew that the only way to attract a guy like this was to make him a founder, so that's what we did."

Performance was going to be critical for Snowflake. In addition to using vectorized query execution, the founders used another method for making the data warehouse ultra-efficient. It's called micro-partitioning. In databases, indexing and partitioning are common techniques used to allow a query to efficiently retrieve data. Indexes create lookup structures that accelerate record retrieval. Partitioning breaks up a table into manageable chunks to focus the data retrieval. Traditional databases require users to manually and explicitly specify indexing and partitioning strategies. The micro-partitioning technique automatically partitions the data in smaller chunks that can be more efficiently targeted. The result is that indexes are not required to deliver industry-leading performance. This technique enabled the Snowflake data warehouse to efficiently handle huge amounts of data, on the petabyte scale, while at the same time making the system easier to use.

Another critical element was simplicity. Late in his years at Oracle, Benoit had become disenchanted with the company's approach to dealing with complexity. Its software was hard to manage. The onus was on customers, or expensive consultants they hired, to constantly tinker with it. He focused on making Oracle's software more self-managing. His goal was to shift the burden from humans to machines.

This was the beginning of a change of orientation for him. He began to understand the need for what he calls "extreme simplicity." By the time he and Thierry were designing the Snowflake data warehouse, Benoit had become an evangelist for making computing as simple as possible for the user. It was to become one of the foundational philosophies for Snowflake.

When Amazon first announced its full public cloud service in 2006, Amazon Web Services (AWS), one of its most remarkable attributes was its ease of use. Customers could visit the AWS Web site, select the services they wanted to use, and pay with a credit card. Benoit and Thierry knew that they needed to design a user interface that would be as simple as Amazon's. It would enable anybody in a company (with permission) to tap into the data warehouse as simply as somebody could sign up for AWS or buy a book on Amazon.

But an easy-to-use interface was the least of their challenges. Databases are extremely complex. In the Oracle world, a customer might employ a team of database administrators (DBAs) to keep each major database working smoothly. Database companies designed elaborate command-and-control systems for DBAs to use to tune the system for each task assigned to it and to deal with problems as they emerged.

The rule at Snowflake was there would be none of this. No "knobs" to adjust. The customers would load their data and they would query their data, but that was it. Behind the scenes, the system would manage itself. If there was a failure, the software would instantly replace failing components—and the end user wouldn't even know it happened.

A key element of simplicity was familiarity. Snowflake hoped to lure customers away from Teradata, Oracle, and IBM, so it would make the migration super-easy. For instance, customers would be able to use the SQL query language, as before. All of the significant changes in the technology would operate in the background, invisible to them. "From the outside, Snowflake smells like any other traditional data warehouse. It's only on the inside that we are fundamentally different," says Benoit.

They designed the architecture for the data warehouse and built its principal features based on their deep knowledge of Oracle's technology and the SQL query language, which was the most popular tool for asking databases for particular bits of information.

THE "DIRTY DOZEN"

By early 2013, the founders had built an engineering team of about a dozen people with the help of Sutter Hill's Doug Mohr. Many of them came from Oracle, but Benoit and Thierry avoided recruiting their friends. "We didn't want them to take the risk based on our friendship," Thierry says. With each new recruit, they had to persuade a person who was enjoying a successful career in another company to leave all of that behind a join a startup that wouldn't have a product to sell for two years. They had to make these strangers believe in the potential of what they were doing as deeply as they believed it themselves.

Those recruiting experiences helped them crystalize their ideas and develop the sales pitch they used when they reached out to investors in their Series B round, in August of 2013. Benoit was worried that they would not be able to raise the money. The early months of Snowflake felt like one of those video games where you play and learn and achieve one level of expertise after another. "To me," Benoit says, "it was incredible that we were still in the game and still continuing." In October of 2014, they raised $20 million in a round led by Redpoint Ventures with Sutter Hill again participating.

The initial product development team—which they nicknamed the "Dirty Dozen"—was a multinational group. Its members hailed from 10 countries. When they gathered at work in the mornings, they would greet each other in their native languages. And they would try greetings in each other's languages. A Russian would try to speak Chinese. A French person would try Urdu. It was a lot of fun. But they also recognized that their strength came in part from their diversity—not just of nationality but of points of view. "It was a culture of everybody's important. It was a culture of helping each other," recalls Marcin, who was born and grew up in Poland. "We wanted people with lots of self-confidence but very little ego." In fact, recruits who proved to have big egos didn't fit, and they left quickly.

In the early days of the company, a culture quickly took shape that was based on the values of the founders. Those values included a focus on teamwork, a belief in egalitarianism, and the desire to think big and to break from computer industry orthodoxy. Nancy Venezia, who was the office manager and employee No. 8, credits the three technical founders with creating a culture that sustained the company for the first couple of years. "We had titles, but they really didn't mean anything," she recalls. "The founders laid the foundation. We were all in it together."

The early employees were excited to be in on the beginnings of something they thought could get really big someday. They called themselves Snowflakes. At that time the company occupied a small office space above a children's play gym in a little brick building near the railroad station in downtown San Mateo.

The culture of the company helped it cope with the inevitable crises that a startup experiences. A key part of data warehouse is the so-called metadata layer—a system for mapping where your core data is stored. Initially, Snowflake's engineers placed their metadata layer in the open source database management system MySQL. But after they began testing their data warehouse they discovered MySQL was incapable of accommodating the massive scale they needed. What to do? This could kill the company. They searched nearly frantically for a solution. It was all hands on deck. Finally, with the help of Sam Pullara of Sutter Hill, they found another open source database, FoundationDB, which had all of the capabilities they were looking for, and more. "It saved Snowflake. We love it," says Thierry.

As CEO, Mike led by example. One of the founding principles at Snowflake was that everybody should feel free to challenge each other's ideas—even those of the executives. Early on, Mike used an all-hands meeting to make his point. He encouraged one of the engineers to disagree with him in public. "I want everyone to see that there are no sacred cows," he says. "You treat everybody with respect, but encourage constructive conflict."

As a result of his years of experience with startups, Mike understood the importance of urgency in a very young company. Everything had to be done quickly, especially software coding—building the product. Mike jokingly urged the programmers to "type faster," and that became a mantra throughout the company. Somebody would talk about a challenge. A colleague would say, "Type faster." It was a joke, but the point was that everyone had to contribute and work fast.

At the same time, Mike encouraged employees to feel free to just be themselves. In the workplace, people often adopt a guarded persona. They don't feel free to express their true nature, which, he believes, impedes their ability to do their best work. So he encouraged people to have fun in the office. For instance, as interim CEO, he worked in the office only two to three days a week, so he didn't have a permanent desk. Each time he arrived, he found a new place to sit. The company was growing so fast that at one point there was no desk for him, so they put him on a futon. On the day of the company Halloween party, members of the team propped a straw dummy on the futon and told Mike he had to work in a broom closet. Later, somebody put Mike's name on a Roomba robotic vacuum cleaner and set it loose on the floor in the office, where it banged into walls and chair legs. The Roomba was programmed to say, "Type faster." Mike says: "It was a way to make fun of the VC and management. I loved the Snowflake culture."

Of course, it was not all fun and games. The young company's list of challenges was far longer than the roster of problems it planned on solving for corporate IT customers. Shortly after Benoit and Thierry started whiteboarding in the apartment in San Mateo, Amazon announced that it was going to offer a data warehouse in the cloud called Redshift. At first, the news made Benoit and Thierry heartsick. But, quickly, they realized that Amazon was placing traditional database technology in the cloud, rather than re-architecting for the cloud like Snowflake. In fact, Amazon's move would validate what they were doing by showing corporations that data warehousing could be done in the cloud.

Another early challenge for Snowflake was the fact that it planned on running its data warehouse *only* in the cloud. There would be no conventional software version that customers could operate on premises, and no "private clouds" where their data would be segregated from the rest. In 2013, most large corporations were not ready to commit to putting their most important data and operations in the public cloud.

REACHING OUT TO CUSTOMERS

Mike and other friends of Snowflake introduced the founders to technical leaders at a number of corporations so they could pitch their concepts to them and get feedback. It was through these conversations that they came to understand how organizations might use their service, and how it might change the way they used data. It became clear that customers would value the ability to have one version of their data that all could tap into—and that their business units and functional organizations would be more willing to share data with one another. Also, since there was no limit on computing and storage, people could get their computing work done quickly, when they wanted to do it.

One of Sutter Hill's core strategies with startups is to not wait until a product is nearly completed to start hiring sales people. They would hire early and send sales people out to make potential customers aware of what was coming but mainly to learn from corporations what they wanted in the product. After every one of these meetings, the Snowflake sales people would send an email to everybody in the company telling what they had learned. In that way, everybody had the same information, unfiltered. This was especially important for the product development team. Mike calls this "collective noise cancellation." He says, "Every engineer could bring to bear their own creativity because they actually understand the problem deeply."

The first sales hire was Chris Degnan, employee No. 16. He had been a district or regional sales manager for most of his nine years in sales management, so he didn't have top-management experience. He had spent many of those years at EMC, the leader in computing storage hardware and software. Chris is not one of those sales guys who can sell anything to anybody. "That's not my style. I have to be passionate about what I sell," he says. "I have to believe in it. I believed in Benoit."

Chris's task at Snowflake was to land the first ten or twenty customers with an unusual proposition: If they gave Snowflake guidance to help develop its product, they would get founding-customer discounts. That meant they would be able to use the product for free initially and later would receive the best discount the company offered. In return, they had to be willing to vouch for Snowflake's technology to the press and other customers.

Initially, Chris spoke to potential customers mainly about the ways that Snowflake's data warehouse would be similar to the on-premises technologies they were used to—except it would be faster and cheaper. "We didn't want to freak them out by talking about all the novel features," recalls Benoit. So Chris didn't focus much at first about the truly differentiating aspects of Snowflake's technology.

Chris identified prospects by searching the job-search website Indeed.com for companies that were hiring engineers with experience in Amazon's AWS cloud platform. Then he and an intern searched by zip code on the professional social networking site LinkedIn for people who listed Amazon RedShift, its cloud data warehouse, as an area of expertise. These were breadcrumbs that led to bakeries—places that might need a cloud data warehouse.

Chris also targeted advertising technology companies, which he knew had a tremendous appetite for Big Data analytics.

The strategy worked. The initial handful of customers were willing to put up with the normal glitches associated with an immature technology. One of the early customers was using a $20 million system to do behavioral analysis of online advertising results. Typically, one big analytics job would take about thirty days to complete. When they tried the same job on an early version of Snowflake's data warehouse, it took just six minutes. After Mike learned about this, he said to himself: "Holy shit, we need to hire a lot of sales people. This product will sell itself."

Well, not quite. But the first two years at Snowflake were driven by boundless optimism that its technology could transform the way organizations use data. At its core, this represented a shared belief in the power of innovation. Thierry sums up the belief this way: "It's important to understand what you don't know yet and what you need to know. The creation comes from imagining what is missing. You need to dream things before you can create things that don't exist."

That's true for technology, and, as Snowflake's story shows, it's true for technology companies, as well.

2

BUILDING THE COMPANY

BOB MUGLIA arrived 10 minutes late for his job interview at Snowflake on May 31, 2014. At the time, the company rented a cramped office, essentially two large rooms, in a small brick building on B Street in San Mateo near the Caltrain station. Bob wasn't familiar with the San Mateo area and he got lost on the way. After he found a parking space, he rushed up a flight of stairs to the second floor and introduced himself by apologizing profusely to Nancy Venezia, the office manager. It was an inauspicious start to what would become a five-year love affair between a man and a company.

Bob had spent much of his career at Microsoft, which was for many years the most powerful company in the computer industry, and, at the end of his stint there, he had run a business that generated more than $15 billion in annual revenues. Now he was considering running a tiny company with fewer than forty employees and zero revenue.

The meetings went well that day—with co-founders Benoit Dageville, Thierry Cruanes, Marcin Zukowski, and the head of sales, Chris Degnan. "I was hooked when Benoit talked about the software architecture," Bob recalls. "It was apparent to me instantly that if the damned thing worked it was going to change the world. At the time, you couldn't be sure it would work, but it was worth a shot."

In a few weeks, Bob signed on to be Snowflake's CEO—employee No. 34. He arrived with a single cardboard box holding a few personal possessions. Nancy pointed him to a desk that was squeezed in among a group of engineers. No problem. Nancy had been concerned when Bob arrived late for his interview, but she liked the fact that he didn't put on airs. She recalls having another thought as well: "Oh boy. Here we go!"

Founding investor Mike Speiser had decided a few months earlier that it was time for him to move on from the interim CEO role, so he and his partners at Sutter Hill had recruited Bob. "I like working with tiny, super-elite teams in engineering and the early stage of sales," Mike says. "But when a company gets ready to launch publicly, I never want to be the face. We need the next level of maturity."

In the summer of 2014, Snowflake was a company with a big idea and a product in development—with a handful of customers testing it. The company was in stealth mode, without even a website, and it would be a year before it officially released its cloud data warehouse.

BUILDING A BUSINESS

Bob's job was straightforward: to turn a ragtag band of software engineers and their handful of business-side colleagues into a real company. It's a classic pivot in the history of most Silicon Valley startups. Typically, at a certain point in the journey, one of the founders or a hired gun like Bob takes on the task of "crossing the chasm" and turning a promising technology into a successful product.

Bob didn't change much at first. He needed to fit in and gain trust. He continued the founders' practice of holding all-hands meetings once a week where the leaders told the rest of the employees what was happening and answered any question anybody wanted to ask. It was such a small, tight-knit group that every new hire would be introduced at an all-hands meeting.

At the time, Benoit and Thierry were essentially co-chief technology officers. Bob asked Marcin to supervise the engineers. Bob was a technical guy and knew a lot about databases and server computers from his years at Microsoft, so he helped out with product management and tuning up the software development process. "Bob's insight into the product and technology were deep," says Marcin. "He could talk to any engineer and understand what they were working on."

Before Bob arrived, the engineering team had faced that technical crisis we mentioned in the previous chapter. They discovered that MySQL, the core database for the metadata in the data warehouse, wasn't capable of scaling up to handle the huge computing tasks the system had to perform. They decided to replace it with a more capable system for doing the job, FountainDB. This meant they had to rewrite much of their software. This process had just begun when Bob arrived.

In those first few months after Bob came on board, he found a culture he was comfortable with—where teamwork and collaboration were paramount. Benoit and Thierry were like yin and yang, always together but with very different personalities. Benoit was outgoing and talkative. He was cool under pressure. In stressful situations he would say, "could be worse." Thierry was quieter, but also calm and collected. In tense moments he would say, "Don't panique," riffing off his native French and elevating the mood. But when he spoke, people listened. Marcin was the resident skeptic. Bob credits Chris with bringing a strong drive for success.

Bob's first task was developing a business model and a pricing scheme. The Snowflake data warehouse initially ran only on Amazon Web Services. Snowflake would purchase raw storage and computing resources wholesale from Amazon, run its software on them, and pass along the costs to its end customers wrapped in its own pricing package. The founders had already made the smart move of charging separately for storage and computing power.

It was clear from the start that Snowflake would mimic Amazon to some extent and bill customers based on how much storage and computing they used. However, Snowflake went well beyond what AWS provided, delivering a data warehouse service that could work with almost unimaginably large amounts of data. Even more importantly, Snowflake could support as many people as needed, all working on the same data at the same time, without interfering with each other. That type of scalability and flexibility was unique in the industry, and Bob put together a business model that was perfectly suited to it. While the model was new to customers, they loved it because it gave them flexibility and saved them money.

The key thing Bob did was abstract pricing from the number of physical nodes (a measure of compute resources) that were to be used to run a given task. Instead, Snowflake would sell computing credits up front that customers would use like money. That way, customers weren't purchasing raw computing power, a commodity; they were paying for value to be received. The credit structure also enabled Snowflake to discount pricing creatively. Initially, they marked up the cost of storage from AWS's base charge of $23 per month per terabyte, but they later switched to essentially making it a pass-through cost, which encouraged customers to aggressively load data into Snowflake. Over time, that policy brought Snowflake more computation business. It took a couple of months to get the pricing model right.

One aspect of the way Snowflake decided to charge customers for services turned computer industry conventional wisdom on its head. Organizations are accustomed to paying more to get their computing jobs done faster. But because Snowflake was so flexible, it could muster enormous amounts of computing power to get things done much faster

—while only charging for the actual compute power used—right down to the second. As Benoit would often say, "faster is free" and customers loved it.

REACHING OUT TO CUSTOMERS

The first paying customer was AccordantMedia, an ad tech company based in New York City. It signed up in July of 2014. (The terms of the deal were negotiated before Bob produced his pricing plan.) At the beginning of that year, Chris had cold-called and sent introductory emails to companies all over the country that were already doing their computing in the cloud. He had reached out to Balaji Rao, Accordant-Media's technology leader:

From: Chris Degnan
Sent: Thursday, January 16, 2014 6:43 PM
To: Balaji Rao
Subject: Cloud Based Data Warehouse Company

Balaji,

I run sales for a Silicon Valley startup called Snowflake Computing (we are stealth mode right now). We have built a standard-SQL based data warehouse platform from the ground up focused on taking advantage of the unlimited resources in the cloud and ease of use for quick business adoption. We are speaking with technology leaders like yourself to get feedback on our platform and its relevance to leading companies like AccordantMedia. We are Series A funded by Sutter Hill Ventures and our founders have years of experience from Oracle, Teradata and other leading data management companies. Please let me know if you have 30 minutes for us to share the details of our platform and its relevance to AccordantMedia and your organization.

Regards,

Chris Degnan
Director of Sales

Balaji had never heard of Snowflake, so he at first ignored the email. Then his boss, who had also received an email from Snowflake, suggested he look at it. He did, and a couple of weeks later, Chris gave him a thirty-minute presentation. "In the first five minutes, I was sold," says Balaji. "Cloud based. Storage separate from compute. Virtual warehouses that can go up and down. I said, 'That's what we want.'"

Before Balaji would try out the Snowflake data warehouse, he wanted a few key features added. Within two weeks, Snowflake's engineers had made the changes and AccordantMedia was running Snowflake—free of charge at first—in parallel with its existing data management technology. With the legacy technology, Balaji had to submit queries on behalf of the company's analysts. With Snowflake, the analysts could write queries themselves and the results came back 10 times faster. "There was a huge demand for analytics in our company. I think of it as the democratization of data," says Balaji. "Snowflake helped us get there."

The data warehouse wasn't stable in those early days, but Snowflake tried to make up for that by smothering early customers with attention. Gordon Wong, who back then ran the data warehousing team for a consumer fitness monitoring company, recalls that merge updates (a method of modifying data in one table in a database based on data from another) were sometimes producing wrong results. After he highlighted the issue, Snowflake put an engineer on the case full-time to partner with Gordon until it was resolved.

At the same time, the sales team had a reputation for not taking no for an answer. Wong recalls negotiating the first contract renewal with Chris, and Chris kept pushing and pushing to get what he wanted. At one point, they were talking on the phone. Gordon was at home. He grew so frustrated that he threw his cell phone across the room. Fortunately, it hit a pillow and didn't break. "In some ways, I admire Chris's hard-headedness," Gordon says. "I admire his courage and tenacity in doing his job, but I was not happy at that moment. If the product wasn't so phenomenal, it could have been a deal-breaker."

Most Silicon Valley tech startups operate in stealth mode for months or years before they announce themselves to the world. They operate that way so they can develop their products and strategies in secret without tipping off eventual competitors that they're gunning for them or without enabling somebody else to steal their idea. By the late summer of 2014, though, the Silicon Valley rumor mill had done its work and others in the tech industry knew what Snowflake was up to. Bob decided it was time to come out of stealth mode. That would make it easier for the company to educate potential customers about its technology and to attract companies willing to try out the beta version of its product.

OUT OF STEALTH MODE

On Oct. 21, 2014, Snowflake sent out its first press release. It announced that it had "reinvented the data warehouse for the cloud." This was a cause for celebration, but nothing over the top—just a wine and cheese party at the office.

There was still a lot of work for the engineering team to do before the product would be ready for prime time. It had to be made "enterprise ready." That meant improving the stability of the service, finishing missing features, eliminating any problems or limitations found by customers, and providing all of the security features required by enterprises like banks and hospitals. They had to be able to encrypt all data in motion and at rest. And they had to provide a Time Travel feature, which allows customers who have problems with their data to dial back to an earlier state that existed before the problems emerged.

Each of their development milestones was named after a run at Northstar California, the ski resort near Lake Tahoe where several of the company's executives had season passes. The last four milestones were Stampede, Challenger, Martis, and Village Run. In early 2015, they turned the weekly all-hands meetings into product shipment progress reports. Everybody in the company was involved. It kept software coders focused on "typing faster." They were driving for the finish line.

It took nearly three years from Snowflake's founding to when it delivered a finished product to the marketplace. This was a powerful cloud service, not some smartphone app, and they were doing technical things that had never been done before. The Snowflake Elastic Data Warehouse became generally available on June 23, 2015.

Not long after the official release, though, came a major outage that shook Bob and the founders—and nearly everybody else in the company. Remember that earlier they had replaced the original database that Snowflake runs on, MySQL, with a database that performed better for them, FoundationDB. But one day in August of 2015, just as the company was about to begin its annual internal sales conference, FoundationDB, too, started to misbehave. The database holds all of the metadata that is necessary to quickly locate data in the data warehouse. It's the heart of the system. "It was going into a death spiral," says Thierry.

The engineering leaders debated whether or not to shut down the entire service—which would be like putting a hospital patient in a coma to save her.

One of the top engineering managers, Jonathan Claybaugh, reached out to Bob on the company's instant messaging system, Slack, when Bob was on his way to speak at the sales conference. He told Bob: "If we shut this down, I don't know if it will ever come back up." The technology team conferred, again on Slack, and Benoit called the shot: Shut it down.

By the time Bob arrived at the venue, he was practically in shock. Chris recalls that Bob was "white as a ghost." Bob told Chris: "We're down and I don't know if we can get back."

Bob struggled through his presentation to the sales team. "It wasn't my best, to say the least," he says. While he spoke, sales people in the audience responded to panicked calls and texts from customers demanding to know what was going on. Chris understood the potential consequences. "If we didn't recover quickly, we would have been screwed," he says. "We would have lost our credibility."

Meanwhile, the technology team assembled a "war room" back at Snowflake's offices, which by this time occupied two floors in a building on San Mateo's Ellsworth Avenue. "This was super-intense," Thierry recalls. Chris remembers that Benoit was usually calm under pressure. "But on that day even Benoit was panicking," Chris says. It took the engineers several hours to understand what caused the problem, to fix it, and to bring the service back on line.

They took a critical lesson away from this near-death experience. They understood more deeply than ever that an always-on cloud service had to be engineered very differently from a traditional on-premises software application. They had to build in features that alerted the data warehouse's self-management system to emergent problems and to build additional capabilities that automatically responded to problems before they could get out of hand.

Another takeaway was the importance of holding customers close—making it clear to them that the relationship wasn't just transactional; it was a true partnership. Like many other startups that cater to enterprise customers, Snowflake established an advisory council made up of representatives from key customers.

In October of 2016, the council convened at Snowflake's headquarters in San Mateo. Erick Roesch, a charter member who worked for an online retailer, recalls that the Snowflake technologists made him feel like he was on their team. He essentially had a backdoor pass to the building. During long working sessions in a conference room, the advisers discussed their frustrations with the product and helped Snowflake engineers set priorities. One pain point was loading data into the warehouse. Another was a problem with the way security was set up. These issues were quickly addressed after the confab ended. "They really did listen," says Roesch. He liked dealing with Snowflake so much that he later went to work there.

Companies typically make decisions about adoption of new technology by inviting a handful of tech providers to compete for their business. Their IT people evaluate the competitors' offerings on paper, narrow the field, and then run cook-offs to see how they perform in real-world situations. Snowflake quickly began to perform well in these head-to-head evaluations.

At game maker Electronic Arts, Vlad Valeyev, chief architect for company operations, recalls that when they compared Snowflake's performance to another competitor's, the results were startling. "It took fifteen to twenty minutes to run queries on the other technology, and five to seven seconds to run the same ones on Snowflake," he says.

Still, getting companies interested in Snowflake was a challenge. A handful of outbound sales people made hundreds of cold calls per day. Typically, the people they reached out to had never heard of Snowflake or even cloud data warehousing. It could be discouraging. Caitlin Griffith, a former yoga instructor who joined the company in 2016, would cook breakfast for the entire sales team on Friday mornings—typically avocado toast with fried eggs on top. The goal was to boost the sales team's morale. Afterwards, they would all cluster their adjustable desks together, raise the surfaces so they could stand in a circle, and hit the phones for an hour. It was a ritual of solidarity and teamwork.

SELLING TO LARGE CORPORATIONS

Large enterprises were especially tough sells. Bob was accustomed to pitching expensive traditional software products to the chief information officers and business leaders of large enterprises, but, in Snowflake's early days on the market, most large corporations weren't ready to move their computing to the public cloud—much less entrust their data to a startup with a funny name that few of them had ever heard of.

When he, the founders, and Chris did get audiences with corporate technology leaders, they ran into one wall after another—including a lot of skepticism about the capabilities of the product itself. "We'd get stopped in the middle of our pitch by a customer who would say, 'I know data warehouses, and what you're saying isn't possible,'" Bob recalls. "I'd smile and tell them, 'Let's go through the architecture,' and I would describe how Snowflake works. When they understood, they would sometimes ask, 'Why doesn't everything work that way?' I'd say, 'it wasn't possible before Snowflake invented it on the cloud.'"

One of the first large companies that granted Snowflake an audience was Goldman Sachs, the big investment banking firm. Benoit, Chris, and one of Chris's sales people made the house call. This was at the end of 2014. At the meeting in New York, Benoit explained the technology, and the Goldman people were impressed. Everything seemed to be going smoothly until someone asked when Snowflake would introduce a version of the technology designed to run in a customer's own data center rather than in the public cloud. Benoit bravely answered: "I predict that you will move your computing to the cloud before we move our technology on premises."

That ended the courtship—for the time being.

One of the Goldman people who attended that first meeting was Matt Glickman, who ran the data platform for the bank's $1 trillion asset management business. While Goldman wasn't ready to commit to Snowflake, Matt was.

He had been at Goldman for more than twenty-four years, and, during that time, he hadn't applied for a single job at another company. But immediately after he walked back to his desk from the meeting, he searched job listings on Snowflake's website. He saw an opening in the marketing department, and, even though he knew little about marketing at the time, he applied for the job. Somebody from Snowflake called him back the next day and asked him what was up. He was clearly a technologist. Did he really want that marketing job? Matt explained that what he wanted was to work for Snowflake. He didn't care what the job was. A few days later, he was on the phone with Bob, and, not too long after that, he was a Snowflake employee. Today, Matt is one of Snowflake's executives, vice president for Snowflake Data Marketplace and customer product strategy.

Goldman became a Snowflake customer exactly three years after the initial sales call.

Like Goldman, Capital One at first rebuffed Snowflake. It was committed to moving to the cloud in a big way but chose another competitor's warehouse initially. Months later, when the other technology proved to be inadequate, Capital One came back to Snowflake. That was a pattern that would repeat itself numerous times in the early years.

Capital One initially came to Snowflake for its ability to separate storage and computing, which allowed the company to run much larger queries and merge and move data in vast quantities quickly.

Capital One ultimately became Snowflake's marquee customer, but it didn't happen overnight. First, Snowflake had to prove itself. After Capital One ran a proof-of-concept test to see if Snowflake's technology could meet its needs, the company handed Snowflake a "to-do" list of additional features it required. In response, Bob and some of Snowflake's technical leaders traveled to Virginia, where Capital One is based. They sat across a table from the bank's technical leaders, including Linda Apsley, who was at the time the bank's vice president for data engineering, discussing the bank's requirements.

Linda and her team provided Snowflake with detailed feedback. Linda recalls that she and Bob sat together to resolve engineering challenges. By November of 2018, they ran a production resiliency exercise based on Linda's feedback—and it worked. "There was cheering on both sides of the country because we knew what had been accomplished," says Linda. She has since left the company.

THE IMPORTANCE OF DATA SHARING

After the release of the "finished" version of the data warehouse in 2015, the work of the engineering team was far from done. If anything, it intensified. Customers asked for additional features. Glitches and faults had to be fixed. And the technology leaders drew up a long road map of new capabilities they wanted to add.

A key one was data sharing—the ability for organizations to easily share with one another just the pieces of information that are relevant. Actually, this capability was present in the technology from the start. When the founders spoke to prospective customers, they would assure security-conscious executives that they had built-in protections to prevent their data from being shared with others. They effectively build firewalls within their cloud. But, eventually, it became clear that the ability to share data securely and conveniently would be a key product differentiator for Snowflake. Once they introduced sharing as a feature and could ensure it was safe, customers went for it.

The sharing was done by essentially poking very precise holes in the firewalls in the data warehouse that separated one company's data from another's. They wouldn't take the data. They would just access it in a transparent and controlled manner consistent with the sensitivity of the data.

The idea of creating a data exchange was a natural outgrowth of the sharing feature. "We saw the impact sharing could have. We thought it could really transform and revolutionize the way data is exchanged," says Benoit.

While it was relatively easy for units within a single enterprise to share data among themselves using the Snowflake data warehouse, the practice was much more difficult when it involved separate organizations. How would one company know that another company might have data that it would be interested in purchasing? The solution was to place a digital catalog on top of the Snowflake data warehouse. Organizations could find each other's data, transact, and share.

That idea grew into Snowflake's second major product category, the data exchange. Engineers began working on the technology in early 2019. The plan was to create a free-to-join marketplace that would enable Snowflake customers to discover data that would be useful to them and query it just like they would query their own data in the Snowflake data warehouse. To make the offer even more attractive to customers, Snowflake decided it would not charge storage fees for customers who accessed others' data in this way.

BUILDING A PLATFORM

It was at this time that Snowflake's leaders began to think about their technology as a platform that other companies could build upon. They knew the power of a technology platform from observing Microsoft. Its Windows computer operating system, first for PCs and later for server computers, was the most powerful software platform in the personal computing era. Thousands of tech companies built applications and tools to run on Windows. Systems integrators developed practices around installing hardware and software. Enterprises based their home-built technologies on it.

Microsoft stood at the center of a sprawling technology ecosystem that exerted powerful gravitational forces not just on technology companies but on every individual and organization that used Windows. And this happened in spite of the fact that many people didn't really like using Windows! That's how powerful a platform can become.

Enterprises and individuals used Windows because it made their lives easier. They could count on getting any software application they wanted, the software packages were interoperable, and the prices were reasonable.

For technology companies, the attraction of Windows was especially strong. While Windows made Microsoft the most valuable and successful company in history for a time, Microsoft shared its success with others. At one point, the company calculated that for every dollar that it made on sales of Windows, seven dollars was generated for its technology partners. Windows was a platform that helped build and sustain an entire industry.

Could Snowflake do something similar? Could it become a powerful platform and foster an industry ecosystem? Bob thought so. During Snowflake's sales conference in 2019, he pitched the idea to the sales team: "The idea of generating more value for the partner or the customer is such a powerful idea because it talks about being a multiplier," he said.

Those partnerships with technology companies were critical. From the beginning, Snowflake has counted on partners to establish and grow its business. The most important partner initially was Amazon's AWS. Snowflake's data warehouse ran on top of it, and the two companies worked closely together to iron out technical conflicts. Later, Snowflake began running on the other two popular public cloud platforms, Microsoft Azure in 2018 and Google Cloud in 2019.

A host of other technology partners helped customers push data into Snowflake and search it for insights. The first analytics company to begin cooperating with Snowflake was Looker, which sells a popular family of business intelligence dashboards. Another important Snowflake early partner was Fivetran, which makes it easy for customers to load data from traditional databases, cloud applications, and other sources into the data warehouse and transform the data into formats that can be easily queried.

THEIR OWN BRAND OF MARKETING

Innovative marketing was essential for a startup like Snowflake, since it competed with some of the giants of the tech industry. In early 2016, Bob had hired Denise Persson as Snowflake's first chief marketing officer. Previously, she had been CMO at Apigee, a San Francisco company that helped enterprise IT organizations build applications using application programming interfaces.

Before her arrival, the company used a typical startup marketing playbook. They bought tiny spaces at the user conferences of larger players, such as AWS. They pitched Snowflake's capabilities to tech industry market researchers in hopes of being mentioned in research reports. And they did all the usual things that startups do on their websites.

Denise changed the game. She introduced a mission for her team, which she called the Five Pillars of Marketing. We won't detail all of the pillars here, but a couple of points bear notice.

The first pillar is to be the most customer-centric team in the cloud computing industry. Every company says it is customer centric, of course, so, what did Denise aim to do differently? It was really about understanding the customers' needs deeply and then educating them about how Snowflake products could make a difference for them.

When Snowflake released its cloud data warehouse in mid-2015, there literally was no cloud data warehouse product category. (Amazon had taken a data warehouse made for on-premises computing and was running it on its public cloud.) The tech industry and enterprise IT departments understood what a data warehouse was but Snowflake's product was a brand new beast. So, on Denise's watch, Snowflake turned itself into something of a book publisher—releasing one short book after another that explained complex topics in simple terms. Example: *Cloud Data Warehousing for Dummies.*

In this way, they not only defined a new product category on their terms; they created an understanding of the key elements that differentiated Snowflake from traditional warehouses and from early cloud competitors. The message was clear: Snowflake was the first data warehouse built from scratch to run in the cloud.

The marketers also made customers and partners the champions of the Snowflake narrative. They published a flood of white papers, blog posts, webinars, and videos that featured customers and partners. The message: It's not about us. It's about you.

The marketing hurdle for Snowflake was even higher than for most tech startups. Others try to persuade corporations to trust their technology to work; Snowflake had to persuade them to trust it with their data, which was quickly being recognized as an extremely important asset for any organization. "You need to establish yourself as the authority, the trusted adviser," says Denise. "You're the nanny for their baby."

At the same time, Denise's marketers weren't afraid to be provocative. They published a book that portrayed competitor Teradata in a very poor light. Its title was *Is That Teradata Box Really Worth $10 Million?* This technique is called poking the bear. It's risky because the bear is bigger than you are and can bite back. In this case, the scheme worked. An executive at Teradata took the bait and penned a series of blog posts firing back at Snowflake. In each post, he included a link to Snowflake's book. "I don't know if he thought of it this way, but, in reality, he was sending hundreds of leads from Teradata's website to ours," says Vincent Morello, Snowflake's chief storyteller.

The company has also attracted notice for its "Snowboards"—billboards it has run along Highway 101 through Silicon Valley and in Chicago and New York. They tend to be cheeky and fun. "LOVE IS BLIND. DATA IS NOT" "YOUR DATA LAKE JUMPED THE SHARK" "DATA WITHOUT BORDERS" "GET AHEAD IN THE DATAPOOL LANE" These billboards didn't come cheap, but they helped put a pint-size company on the tech industry map.

RAISING BOATLOADS OF CASH

From his early days at CEO, Bob knew that raising money from venture capitalists would be one of his most important jobs. That's because Snowflake's product was large and complex, which would require a lot of high-quality engineers and would have to be sold primarily through a field sales force. Bob had to hire quickly and keep hiring. Also, Snowflake was competing with tech giants that had practically unlimited funds, so it had to develop breakthrough technologies, tell its story aggressively, and sell fast to get out ahead of them. Bob had never raised money from VCs before, so he took a lot of advice and hands-on help from Mike, Snowflake's founding investor.

There's a rule of thumb coined by venture capitalist Neeraj Agrawal of Battery Ventures: "Triple, triple, double, double, double." It's the idea that highly successful Software-as-a-Service startups should triple revenues in each of their first two years with a product on the market and double revenues in each of the next three years. Snowflake was on track to go triple-triple-triple.

Snowflake was in the middle of a land rush. The more customers it got, the more data it got, and the more data it got, the harder it would be for competitors to dislodge it. Bob felt the company had to grow fast in every dimension. All of that growth had to be fed by cash from venture capitalists. "We were in a land-grab environment and nobody was telling us to slow down," recalls Bob. During his five years as CEO, he raised more than $900 million.

Raising money wasn't always easy, though. In early 2016, Bob and Mike began to raise a round of funding from venture capitalists. It was an extension of the C-round. The stock market had suddenly weakened. The S&P Index plummeted 10 percent in just two weeks. Investors were jittery—including venture capitalists. Bob practically had doors slammed in his face. The company was burning cash fast and needed more. It was saved, essentially, by Sutter Hill, which invested and persuaded other Snowflake investors to ante up again—this time at a flat valuation.

Crisis averted. After that, as Snowflake's revenues and reputation soared, it became easier to raise money. In October of 2018, Bob raised a whopping $450 million in one shot.

Snowflake was riding high. It had a roster of more than 1,000 customers, including new ones with strong brand names such as Netflix, Office Depot, and Yamaha.

Looking back on Bob's tenure as CEO, Benoit praised him. "Thierry and I were passionate about our vision for Snowflake, but we lacked the business acumen of knowing how to scale a team," he said. "When we brought on Bob, everything changed. He had incredible experience and ingenuity, and he fully embraced Snowflake from the very start. His pride and passion for Snowflake was infectious and it took the company to new heights."

BOB'S DEPARTURE

Bob managed Snowflake's pell-mell growth well for more than four years. But as time went on, the company grew bigger and more complex. The board wanted to be sure it had the executives and and business processes in place to bring Snowflake to the next level—so it could maximize its potential and investors could maximize their return on investment. In the spring of 2019, the board decided to replace Bob as CEO. It's not unusual for boards to change leadership for any number of reasons.

The unusual thing about Snowflake's situation was the company was doing so well at the time. The board felt a new stage of growth required new leadership.

On May 1, 2019, the board issued a press release thanking Bob for his service. Bob approved a quote: "It has been an honor and a privilege to lead the Snowflake team over the past 5 years as we have built the world's best cloud data warehouse. Our success is founded upon our values, the foremost of which is putting the customer first."

In a separate press release, the board announced that Frank Slootman would be the new CEO. In his statement, he called Snowflake a special company: "There is a lot of software running in the cloud but very little of it fully exploits its scale, performance, elasticity and economics. Snowflake does, and it is poised to become the leading data platform of the cloud era."

3

SNOWFLAKE TODAY

A FEW DAYS after Frank Slootman took over as CEO of Snowflake in May 2019, he conducted his first all-hands meeting. Mike Speiser and two other members of the board of directors joined him. About 300 people gathered in an auditorium-like room at headquarters, and hundreds more dialed in via a Zoom videoconference.

Frank recalls the message he sent: "I said, 'Look. I'm here to run the business. As the CEO, I only have one job and that is to increase the value of the franchise. It's not about profits or revenues, per se. The investors want to maximize what their investment is potentially worth.'"

He also warned that competition was about to get tougher. They were going up against giants of the tech industry. "You're going to get a war," he said. "It's coming for you. You better get your boots on."

Listening to Frank talk about running a company is like getting a master class in operational excellence. He has been through the process of building a company to maturity enough times that he has granite-like views on just about any leadership topic you could imagine.

His business career started in his native Netherlands, where he felt corporate leaders were too soft, not aggressive enough. Eventually he found his way to Silicon Valley, where there is no shortage of aggression.

He held management positions at Compuware, a leading mainframe computing software maker, and Borland Software, a developer tools company. Then, as CEO, he led two companies through the early and middle stages of development. The first was Data Domain, a pioneer in using disk storage for backup and recovery. Data Domain almost single-handedly made the tape automation industry, which had owned backup and recovery since the beginning of computing, obsolete. Next came ServiceNow, which sells workflow automation systems for managing a range of business processes, from IT to HR to customer service. In both cases, he took the companies public. They were wildly successful.

In the months after Frank became CEO of Snowflake, a dozen or so people who had worked for him at ServiceNow and at Data Domain came to work for him. He calls himself "an acquired taste," but a lot of people like his style. One Snowflake executive observes: "Where Frank goes, people make money. But, also, a lot of people really love working for him."

THE THREE STAGES OF COMPANY BUILDING

Frank believes tech startups have three stages of development before they become mature. The first stage is embryonic. It's a small team of engineers, heads down, building a product. This stage lasts a year or two, maybe even three, until the founders are ready to test their product in the marketplace.

The second stage is the formative one. Will customers buy the product? What will they pay for it? Will the business model work? Basically, you figure out how to turn the organization into a functioning business. You burn a ton of cash. There is less concern about efficiency at this stage. In fact, working for a company in this stage can feel quite chaotic. This is also the stage most startups never exit.

The third phase is scale. This is where Snowflake is. You focus on growth first and foremost, then efficiency, cash flow, and unit economics. You have to find the right balance. These factors are especially important for a company like Snowflake, a cloud technology vendor that gets paid for services when they are consumed by the customer. That's in stark contrast to traditional software companies, which typically receive huge license payments up front and then sizable annual maintenance fees. It's also different from the Software-as-a-Service business model. Customers pay monthly fees to SaaS companies—whether they use the service a lot or not. "We're not a SaaS company in economic terms, so we can't spend like one," Frank says. "We have to be far more efficient and disciplined."

During his first week on the job, Frank met with each of his direct reports, one on one. The board had agreed that he would appoint two executives he had worked with at previous companies—Mike Scarpelli as CFO and Shelly Begun as head of human resources. By bringing in people he knew who would operate without much direction, he could focus on a narrower scope of remaining challenges. He retained Denise Persson as chief marketing officer and Chris Degnan as chief revenue officer. He asked Benoit to become president of products, hired Greg Czajkowski from Google to run engineering and support, and moved other chess pieces around—or out. Things were in flux for a while. Frank went from having fifteen direct reports when he joined to just five a few weeks later.

Greg had worked at Google for fourteen years and was running a large product engineering group building data analytics infrastructure for all of Google as well as products for Google Cloud. In particular, the group produced BigQuery, Google's competitor to Snowflake's cloud data warehouse. It was a huge coup for Snowflake to land Greg. "We needed him,"

Frank says. "While we had tremendous creative and innovative muscle in engineering, we lacked the ability to scale, mature, and harden our cloud platform and our organization. It was unfocused, with different factions pursuing different ideas of the company priorities."

You are probably getting the idea by now that Frank Slootman is a no-nonsense guy. He starts off every executive team meeting with what he calls a "lightning round." Each executive quickly tells the others what they need to know about what's going on in their area, and why they need to know about it. If people have nothing important to say, they say nothing.

One of the key messages he sent to the executives who didn't know him was that he is a "lateral operator," not a hierarchical one. He didn't want them to come to him to arbitrate their differences. He wanted them to take responsibility and to resolve matters among themselves. They should come to him only if they could not work things out. The same approach should be adopted throughout the organization. He wanted people at each level to work closely with their counterparts in other functions and departments. Just like there should be no data silos in an enterprise, there should be no operational silos.

Frank calls himself a "malcontent" and nurtures that sentiment in other people. He cringes when people talk about how proud they are of themselves or the companies they work for. "Pride signals satisfaction with the status quo," he says. "I focus on the distance from where we are to where we can and need to be."

Frank brought a top-down leadership style to the company, like Steve Jobs at Apple. He did not seek to change Snowflake's values. Put Customers First. Integrity Always. Think Big. Be Excellent. Get It Done. Own It. Embrace Each Other's Differences. These were values that had been established over the years, and Frank embraced them. Yet Frank wasn't fond of the idea of just putting values posters up on the office walls. Rather, he intended to "prosecute them," he says. "You prosecute values every moment of the day. Every meeting, every interaction, every situation is an opportunity to enforce values." He believes that values are just feel-good statements of intent until you work up the courage to act on them.

Numerous people said they were shaken at first by the sudden change in leadership—and leadership style—but they gradually came around. "It hasn't been an easy transition. It took time to process through it," says Joshua Skarphol, a consultant in Snowflake's professional services organization. "That being said, I think it's time now to put on our big-boy pants and move into the future that we're all hoping to achieve."

For example, the professional services organization started off in 2017 with the mission of helping customers get the maximum value out of the data warehouse, beginning with training. Most of the services were ad hoc—and many were free. Revenue was mostly an afterthought. That changed. The professional services organization now goes to market with a menu of well-defined offerings, each with a price tag.

HOW TO SCALE A COMPANY

Frank has three rules for the "scaling" phase of company building:

RULE 1: Increase velocity. Organizations generally move way slower than they can and should. Leaders set the tempo. If they act like they're the boss of the local state Department of Motor Vehicles office, employees settle into that glacial pace. To change things, leaders have to radically shift expectations. If somebody asks, "Can I get it to you next week?" you might answer: "How about tomorrow morning?"

The new expectations cascade through the organization, vertically and horizontally. Soon, everybody is moving faster. The new pace starts to feel normal, and you don't have to constantly remind people anymore. "Every organization has its own pace, and intensity, and energy level, and I work to amp that up all the time," says Frank.

RULE 2: Raise standards. Everybody in an organization should learn to expect more of themselves and of those around them. Steve Jobs is the inspiration here. At Apple on his watch, an idea or a design or a strategy had to be "insanely great." Otherwise, it was worthless. Frank believes that a lack of mental discipline causes people in organizations to operate in the "good enough" mode. "It's not the C players that kill organizations. It's easy to spot them. It's the B players. They destroy you with mediocrity," he says.

Frank advises employees to go home at night and look in the mirror. They should ask themselves: "Was it important, even essential, that I was working there today? Did I matter and make a difference for the organization?" If the answer is no or not conclusive, they need to step up and demand more from themselves. "We'll try to help people, but it's a mindset we want people to try on, no matter how uncomfortable that may be," he says. "People will inevitably feel better about themselves and more secure in their positions when they raise their own bar."

RULE 3: Narrow your focus. Frank believes that one of the causes of "good enough" behavior is that people have too much on their plates. Whether they are executives, managers, or individual contributors, people try to do too many things at once. That may work for high-performance computers, but it is rarely effective for individuals. People may feel like they're being productive, but they're running in circles.

Instead, Frank believes, employees should develop a strong sense of priorities. Choose the things that are most important to get done in a given slice of time. Then apply yourself intensely to those tasks, serially, in rank order, until the tasks are done. He believes that by operating in this way people will produce better results and complete tasks quicker. When he arrives at a company, he often removes responsibilities from executives rather than piling them on. "My role is to create blinding clarity about what's important," he says.

When Frank arrived at Snowflake, the company was doing fantastically by many measures. Revenue growth was strong. In fact, revenue would more than double during the fiscal year in which he took over. Snowflake had a great reputation with customers and the press. It still had more than $500 million in the bank. And its cloud service was handling hundreds of millions of data queries per day from customers.

In other ways, though, Snowflake was off track. Frank says he found "a company that was struggling to do things as an organization." The main trouble spots were in the general and administrative functions— and across the board in runaway spending and staffing. "Nobody had given much thought to efficiency, yield, leverage—and the profit-and-loss statement showed it," he says.

Mike Scarpelli, who was Frank's CFO at ServiceNow and Data Domain, came in with a mandate to reshape the financial side of the business. His first priority was to instill financial discipline, normalize expenses, and root out waste. He looked at all of Snowflake's costs through a forensic lens. For instance, he examined the use of software from other tech companies. He found that in many cases, Snowflake was paying for software licenses that it did not actually use. He tore up some software contracts and consolidated others. "There was a lot of freedom among business functional managers to just go out and buy whatever they thought they needed," Mike says. He put an end to that.

He also worked with Chris Degnan to change the compensation scheme for the sales force. Previously, field sales people would be paid commissions up front when they landed a deal. That meant they got paid long before Snowflake did. Now they get half of their compensation up front and the other half spread over the term of the contract, based on the level of usage. This creates alignment between compensation and what the company needs from its sales staff. One of the goals of the switch is to give sales people an incentive to expand the use of Snowflake within an organization—to develop a long-term relationship—rather than skipping from one customer to the next in rapid succession. The strategy is called "land and expand."

At the same time, Chris reorganized the sales team. In the past, many field sales people were assigned to handle a basket of customers ranging in size from 200 employees to 1 million. The new structure created a separate field sales organization focusing on the 250 largest accounts, called majors, and another that handles the bulk of the field-sales customers, called the enterprise team. People in the majors group might be assigned to four or five customers; those in the enterprise group might have thirty to forty. Snowflake had to shift gears to going after the largest customers in the world, and its high-volume, transactional selling model did not fit the task. Landing very large customers can take years and requires different skills, people, compensation approaches, contracts, pricing, and so on.

A third group, the corporate sales team, reaches out to sales prospects via the phone and email. That team focuses on companies with fewer than 200 employees. Many are tech companies. The goal is not only to get their data on Snowflake but also to persuade them to build their applications on top of Snowflake's data platform.

In keeping with the new sense of urgency in the company, Chris did not wait until the end of the fiscal year to do the reorg. He did it in the middle of the year. As a result of the maneuver, all the sales territories in North America changed, and thousands of customers got a new sales person assigned to them. He later described the move as "open heart surgery without the painkillers."

The overhaul was disruptive but worth it, says Carlin Eng, a sales engineer in the enterprise sales group. Frank had warned at a gathering of his team that just because revenues were growing so fast, they should not become complacent. They had to serve customers more effectively and operate more efficiently. "People joke that the product sells itself, but there's a danger in that," Carlin says. "The message was that we'll be in trouble if we're not really disciplined and diligent about making sure we're doing things the right way."

There were changes to come on the human resources side, as well. Shelly Begun, who ran HR for Frank at ServiceNow and Data Domain, says she has always felt like a "Martian" in the HR function. "I don't align with what I call the adult daycare version of HR," she says. "I think HR should be very business-centric and operate more in the white spaces rather than imposing bureaucratic controls on the organization."

It all goes back to one of Frank's core beliefs—that managers should be accountable for solving their own problems as much as possible. HR should not get in the way. Rather, it should do its best to clear obstacles from managers' paths. Take hiring and onboarding of new employees: According to Shelly, this should be handled with the minimum of form-filling and unnecessary interviews with HR people. HR is there to support, not to control.

Shelly and Frank also have unconventional views on annual performance reviews. They're against them. Managers should communicate with their people directly and immediately when they need supervision or deserve praise, but they should not spend time on lengthy reviews. Snowflake now has a quarterly bonus program. Managers within a function get together in a room, assess the performance of members of their teams, and deal out bonuses to individuals based on their judgment as a group. Then the managers meet with employees one on one and give them direct feedback about their performance.

When it's time to part ways with someone, Snowflake does not force people to endure a long and torturous process. Supervisors are not required to document an employee's every deficiency, and employees are not pressured into participating in performance-improvement programs. "That's demeaning. It's inhuman," Shelly says. "We sit down with the person and tell them it's not working out. We are all employed 'at will,' from the CEO on down. Then we give them a runway to find their next job."

While Frank and Shelly's approach to HR may diverge from the touchy-feely spirit that pervades many companies in Silicon Valley, a number of Snowflake employees said they found it refreshing.

A NEW STYLE OF COMMUNICATIONS

While Frank believes in fulsome communications with employees, he does not believe in frequent all-hands meetings. He expects line managers to be the principal communicators. When he came onboard, the company was conducting all-hands meetings every month. He switched that to quarterly, like a public company typically does.

Caitlin Griffith, who heads the field marketing team and has been at Snowflake since 2016, was wary of the new approach at first. She wondered if Snowflake would continue to feel like a close-knit company. But she has grown accustomed to Frank's style, and she likes it. "Frank flows information from his direct reports down to us," she says. "I think that chain of information is very scalable and effective. Also, if I want to know something, I can get my hands on it within a matter of thirty minutes."

At the quarterly all-hands meeting on December 12, 2019, all the awkwardness and apprehension of Frank's first all-hands gathering were gone. Dressed casually in jeans and a navy-blue sweater, he faced a lively crowd of 300 people, mostly in their twenties and thirties, speaking with the ease of a stand-up comedian. He even cracked a few jokes. And people laughed.

After other executives discussed finances, the sales reorg, and technical matters, Frank said he wanted to talk about organizational change. The company was growing fast. It had 1,600 employees and expected to add 1,000 in the next year. "The more people come in, working together gets harder," Frank said. "We have to think more about how we operate. There are things we can do every day, in every conversation and in every project. I call this everyday choices."

Frank clicked the projector remote control, and the company's eight corporate values flashed onto the screen behind him. This day's homily was about one of the values—Own It.

First, he told people in the crowd that he wants them to stop operating in functional silos. If they have a problem with something another group is doing, they should resolve it by going directly to the person they have a problem with and work things out. They should not escalate to their boss unless they exhaust the direct approach.

Then he told them not to "delegate up." They should make routine decisions, and even some difficult ones, on their own. "We delegate down in this organization, not up," he said, eliciting a smattering of laughter.

Last, he talked about appropriating authority—the habit people have of citing the opinions of tech market research groups or even Frank, himself, when taking a position in a meeting. He urged them, instead, to bring their own data and analysis. "Don't assert my authority; assert yours," he said. "You're shutting down conversation when you do that. You have to win an argument based on your own authority. Kill that reflex. Own it."

People in the audience took Frank's urgings to heart. For instance, Saqib Mustafa, the head of the partner marketing team, began interacting more directly and routinely with the product marketing team. From time to time, pre-COVID, he simply found an empty desk in the pod where the other group sat, plopped down, and started working—which inevitably led to conversations. He also invited people from the other group to sit with his group. These interactions paid off in innumerable and immeasurable ways. "Talking face to face resolves so many things," Saqib says. "When we're bringing in people and building teams, we have to make sure we're all still living our values and our culture."

SNOWFLAKE 2.0

When Frank made Benoit president of products, it wasn't a symbolic gesture designed to show respect to the founders and rekindle warm feelings among longtime employees. He put Benoit in charge of engineering, product management, and technical support. He wanted the same kind of bold technical thinking that Benoit and Thierry had launched the company with seven years earlier. And he got it.

The odd thing was, Benoit had never had a management role at Snowflake. He had been the chief technology officer, essentially, from the start. He wasn't even that comfortable with managing. But he took on his new responsibilities with energy and enthusiasm. He says: "I *own* the product, the way it is day to day and the way it will be for the years going forward—the vision."

He came up with a vision he calls Snowflake 2.0. Most technology startups, even if they're successful, never develop a second act. They're one-hit wonders, at best. Snowflake wants to keep developing mind-blowing capabilities. After Benoit got his new assignment, he took the company's ideas about being a data analytics platform and turned them into a comprehensive technology strategy and a product-development road map. Snowflake would expand its technical capabilities in multiple directions, all with the aim of establishing itself as the world's preeminent cloud data platform.

What AWS had become for cloud computing infrastructure, Snowflake would be for the Data Cloud.

In Snowflake's earliest days, Benoit, Thierry, and the rest of the engineering team did some amazingly original work, creating a brand-new software architecture for managing data. Then there was a period when they focused on making their software enterprise-ready—stable, secure, and packed with the features that large customers demand. With the launch of Snowflake 2.0, they were back where they started, in a sense. It was a time again for exploration and bold acts of innovation.

The cloud data platform they were building would include major new elements, including a pipeline for bringing all kinds of data types into the warehouse, innovative data search, and data exchanges for enabling companies to more easily share, buy, and sell data. The engineering team would also add features that would make it easier for enterprises to ingest different kinds of data, manage it, and analyze it. Think of the cloud data platform as a process that converts data from raw materials into finished products—from iron ore into Ferrari.

Snowflake introduced its cloud data platform at AWS's re:invent conference in Las Vegas on December 2, 2019.

The cloud data ecosystem diagram shows how the most significant elements of a cloud data platform fit together—and how they fit within a broader cloud data ecosystem, which includes data sources and data consumers. The cloud data platform includes pieces provided by Snow-

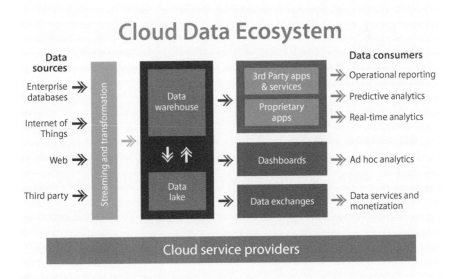

Cloud Data Ecosystem

Data sources
- Enterprise databases
- Internet of Things
- Web
- Third party

Streaming and transformation

Data warehouse

Data lake

3rd Party apps & services

Proprietary apps

Dashboards

Data exchanges

Data consumers
- Operational reporting
- Predictive analytics
- Real-time analytics
- Ad hoc analytics
- Data services and monetization

Cloud service providers

flake, technology partners, data partners, and customers. (The cloud data platform technologies are the boxes in the middle.)

On the left side of the diagram, you see the main sources of data—structured, semi-structured, and unstructured. The types include data from an organization's run-the-business software applications and traditional databases; information from the Web including emails and click data; information gathered from Internet of Things (IoT) devices, including smartphones; and data from third-party providers, such as weather and financial markets information.

Data is typically ingested into the Snowflake data warehouse through a mechanism called Snowpipe. That's a staging area through which data is streamed continuously and, in some cases, transformed on the fly, so it can be accessed easily once it is in the data warehouse. Today, many corporate IT departments load data into their data warehouses once a week or once a day, in batches. That means their data is stale before they can even analyze it. With Snowpipe, customers can bring in data continuously. No waiting around.

Customers use specialized tools for ingesting data and performing data transformations, including a function known as Extract, Transform, Load (ETL). A variant of this approach is ELT, which stands for Extract, Load, Transform, where data is loaded into the data warehouse before it is transformed. Snowflake collaborates closely with a number of ETL and ELT companies, including Informatica, Fivetran, and Matillion. In addition, other companies provide specialized data services for enterprise customers. Say a customer wants to analyze historic records tracking manufacturing quality or customer interactions, but in earlier times the data was organized differently. A data service company will convert the data so it is all compatible.

The Snowflake data platform is being enhanced so it can handle unstructured data, such as articles in scientific journals, medical images, and videos. This data is not stored directly in the data warehouse, but metadata about it is stored there, so it is easily searchable.

To the right of the data warehouse in the diagram, you see the technologies and methods that are used to access and analyze data.

Hundreds of analytics applications and tools created by software makers are built on top of Snowflake's technology or tap into the data warehouse. Among them are a new wave of artificial intelligence companies, including DataRobot and Dataiku. There are dashboards for monitoring and viewing data, like those from Looker and Tableau. Snowflake now has its own dashboard, as well, which makes it easy for data analysts to quickly create gadgets for keeping track of business events and trends, and for receiving alerts.

Snowflake's cloud data platform enables enterprise customers to find applications and tools from partners that might be useful to them. On Snowflake's website, Partner Connect is like Apple's App Store. Customers can browse a wide variety of products. If they want to try one out, they spin up a data warehouse with the application running on it. Instantly, with no need for configuration, they can do a test drive using their own data.

Also in the diagram, you see the proprietary analytics technologies built by enterprise IT departments and systems integrators. They use programming languages, query languages, and software frameworks to access and manage data and data processing. Those technologies include SQL, which is the lingua franca of data analytics. Another one, Apache Spark, enables organizations to write programs using a variety of languages that efficiently use clusters of computers to perform real-time analytics of huge sets of data.

Increasingly, enterprises and the companies that supply technology to them are using artificial intelligence tools to draw insights from a variety of data sources and types. Machine learning, for instance, enables them to understand what is happening in their businesses (and in their computing systems) more deeply by learning from events and interactions with the data. Rather than requiring analysts and business leaders to always think of the right questions to ask the data, learning systems can provide answers to questions they have not asked—or even thought of. In these scenarios, the information made available in the data warehouse can be consumed by people or computing systems, or both.

On the bottom of that stack of boxes, you see data exchanges. They enable organizations to list data in online catalogs, handle transactions, and facilitate sharing. This is where companies can find and purchase third-party data they need to provide further context around the data they own. It's a platform for data commerce.

WHAT COMES NEXT?

Many of the pieces of Snowflake 2.0 are already in place and are being used by thousands of customers. Others are still on the drawing boards. Benoit and his team are collaborating closely with technical leaders and customers to identify needs, set priorities, and design features and the technologies that support them.

It's an ambitious vision requiring an immense amount of innovation, but Benoit says he feels comfortable leading the initiative because of the accomplished technologists clustered around him. They include Thierry as CTO, Greg Czajkowski as head of engineering, and Christian Kleinerman as head of product management and design.

Greg remembers the first time he was aware of Snowflake. He was driving on Route 101 through Silicon Valley and he saw one of those cheeky Snowflake billboards. He doesn't remember what it said, but he recalls thinking it was a gutsy move to enter the space already inhabited by several giants of the industry—including his employer at the time, Google.

Over a few years, he watched as Snowflake gained momentum in the marketplace. As an engineer, he was impressed with Snowflake's technology. He also observed that while Amazon, Microsoft, and Google were able to include technologies in their clouds that provided advantages for their data warehouse products, Snowflake did not have that ability. But he says Snowflake more than made up for it with superior design. "Snowflake had no access to those special resources, so it had to be awesome at the art of creating really high-performance database systems," he says.

Like Greg, Christian had worked at Google before coming to Snowflake. After he arrived, he came to understand more deeply than before the growing importance of data in business and the economy. Businesses need a tremendous amount of data, they need a wide variety of data types, and they need it all fast—so they can make timely decisions. "People will tell you that if they had to choose between having more data or having better algorithms, they'd choose more data every time," he says. "It's the data that leads to better predictions." Christian sees Snowflake, with all of its data management capabilities, as a strategic partner for organizations seeking to maximize the value of their data assets.

As Snowflake 2.0 took shape, the race was on to innovate and turn the vision of the cloud data platform into full-blown reality.

One of the first steps along that path was the Snowflake data exchange. Frank announced the product at the company's first-ever user conference, Snowflake Summit, which it hosted in San Francisco a little more than a month after he joined. Staging a first-user conference is something of a rite of passage for technology companies. It shows the world that you have enough gravitational pull to attract thousands of customers who are willing to spend a couple of days and one or two thousand dollars to hear you tell them how great your product is.

The data exchange is a free-to-join marketplace that enables Snowflake customers to easily discover and purchase data from third-party providers, and then view it from within their Snowflake accounts. A private version of the exchange, allowing organizations to share data with a select group of partners or individuals within their business ecosystems, was introduced six months later. You'll learn much more about data exchanges in Chapter 7.

A second critical step in building out the platform is making it truly global. The large cloud vendors, AWS, Microsoft Azure, and Google, actually operate a number of separate clouds for different geographies. For instance, each typically has one cloud for the western half of the United States and another for the eastern half. Many companies, even relatively small ones, operate globally. Using regional clouds is fine if each of their global business units organizes its computing and its data regionally or nationally. But these days, a lot of the value in cloud data analytics comes from combining data from around the globe so an organization has a single integrated view of its business activities. Because of the way the large public clouds are structured, global companies cannot easily get the single view they want.

That's why Benoit and the team launched a major initiative, called Snowflake Global, aimed at creating a globally distributed data cloud. This technology, which involves replication and syncing of data, makes it possible for customers to operate what looks to them like a single global instance of the Snowflake data warehouse. They can view and query data using any regional cloud as their point of entry. The technology also enables customers to run data warehouses on more than one of the public clouds. That frees them from being overly dependent on a single cloud provider—AWS, Microsoft Azure, or Google.

When the founders first conceived of the cloud data warehouse, they felt it was vital to make it easy to use by business analysts and database administrators who were steeped in the lore of the traditional database. That meant focusing on the tried-and-true SQL query language. But as data analytics evolved, a new generation of analysts and data scientists emerged. These people write data analytics applications using the Python, Java, or Scala programming languages to draw insights from large quantities of diverse data. Their queries are typically more complex, often involving machine-learning algorithms.

To respond to this type of user, Snowflake's engineers at first developed tight technology integrations with the new programming languages and tools, including the popular Apache Spark data analytics engine. There was a hang-up, though. Data scientists working for customers had to pull data out of Snowflake to run it through their programs. That requires extra steps and defeats the purpose of having a single version of data. So, Benoit and his team set out to develop technologies that will enable data scientists to run their programs on data while it sits inside the data warehouse.

In addition, they began designing technologies to enable "citizen data scientists" to run machine-learning-powered analytics programs within the data platform. These are business analysts who do not have the programming expertise of a data scientist but are capable of formulating sophisticated data queries—those used to forecast demand for products or to spot sentiment patterns in online product reviews, for instance. The goal is to democratize data science.

They also went to work to address the streaming data challenge. These days, a torrent of data from Internet of Things sensors streams into enterprise computer systems. Much of it piles up in huge "data lakes," where it's not immediately actionable. Snowflake's engineering team is developing technologies that make it easier to combine streaming IoT data with other data types within the data warehouse and analyze it in near-real time, so humans or machines can react to the results in a matter of seconds. For instance, with capabilities like this, energy utility companies can more easily combine live demand data with weather reports to help them keep the optimum mix of wind, solar, and natural gas-generated electricity. And they can make contingency plans as a major storm approaches.

BLACK DIAMOND

Some of these Snowflake 2.0 technologies have already come to market. Others are works-in-progress. Still others are little more than pipe dreams. One way that Benoit and his team set priorities and make design decisions is by seeking the advice of members of Snowflake's customer advisory council, called the Black Diamond Executive Council.

Early in 2020, Snowflake staged a three-day Black Diamond event at a resort on the outskirts of Scottsdale, Arizona. The desert was beautiful, with monumental saguaro cacti and mesquite bushes the size of small houses seeming to pose, postcard-like, among the rock-pile hills. But Snowflake executives and seventeen guests spent little time admiring the scenery. They engaged with one another almost continuously from 7 in the morning until 10 at night, discussing such things as Spark-like programming models, SQL extensions, data governance, and data pipelines.

These user-council confabs are incredibly valuable for the host companies. Snowflake's engineering leaders are able to float ideas to see if they will meet customer needs—and get immediate and detailed feedback. At the Arizona event, they taped posters on the walls representing a mix of technology initiatives and customer pain points. They invited council members to place Post-It notes on the items that were most important to them. Then they tallied up the totals to help set priorities.

During this same exercise at the previous Black Diamond meeting, feedback from advisers prompted the engineering team to change course on strategy for the data exchange. This time, it was more of an affirmation of paths Snowflake was already on.

At breakfast on the third day, Matt Glickman, vice president for Snowflake Data Marketplace and customer product strategy, mulled over what he had learned. "The big takeaways were the concrete things about what it takes to be a data platform," he said. "We're going to make more of the building blocks."

He was sitting at a large round table with a group of advisers. The corporate technology leaders who join councils like this tend to be fans, but they do not typically drink the Kool-Aid. This is an opportunity for them to shape the direction of technologies that could have significant impacts on the companies they work for, not to mention the trajectories of their own careers. When they have something critical to say, they do not mince words. From time to time, though, members of the Black Diamond council say things that make Snowflake executives feel like the rain clouds have parted and the sun is shining through. This was one of those times.

Ravi Poruri, head of data and business intelligence for a leading cloud storage company, sat opposite Matt at the table. He took a sip of coffee and set his cup down. "In Snowflake, I see another Salesforce in the making," he said. He was referring to the SaaS company that dominates not only the customer relationship management software market but also the skyline of San Francisco, with its gleaming office tower. "Salesforce was the first enterprise cloud company," Ravi said. "Snowflake is the first data platform built on the cloud."

Just a few weeks later, Snowflake announced a wide-ranging strategic partnership with Salesforce, which included an investment by the SaaS giant.

Here comes the sun.

4

HOW SNOWFLAKE USES ITS OWN TECHNOLOGY

BACK IN 1988, Microsoft executive Paul Maritz sent an email to one of his subordinates titled "Eating our own Dogfood." He was concerned that the company was not aggressively adopting one of its own products, the not-yet-popular LAN Manager networking software package. He wanted Microsoft to show more confidence in its own networking expertise.

After that, the phrase spread like wildfire across Microsoft as it moved from one software market after another—and then to other tech industry companies.

Paul made a compelling argument. Why would a tech company expect customers to buy its product if the company itself wasn't using it extensively? Beyond the confidence issue, it makes sense for the engineers who are designing a product to have a first-hand customer experience—starting during the alpha- and beta-testing phases of product development. That way, they learn from their mistakes.

Snowflake has been eating its own dog food since it uploaded the first test version of its data warehouse to the Amazon Web Services cloud in 2014. Today, the Snowflake cloud data platform has become the technology foundation upon which the company runs its business. It is known as "Snowhouse" internally. Says CEO Frank Slootman: "Snowhouse is the beating heart of Snowflake. The entire definition of what we are and we do is there."

Since Snowflake is a data-driven company, and data analytics is an essential part of everything it does, it's no surprise that every major group iin the company, from engineering to sales to marketing to finance, is taking advantage of its own technology.

When Sunny Bedi reported for duty in January 2020 as Snowflake's first-ever chief information officer, he found an organization that was testing the limits of its own technology but wasn't doing it in a disciplined way. Snowflake, the organization, was kind of like a puppy—house-trained but still rambunctious. Each group within the company used the technology the way it suited them, without central guidance and coordination.

Sunny had previously been head of IT at NVIDIA, a leader in high-performance microprocessor technology. He joined NVIDIA in 2008 when it was in a similar developmental stage to what Snowflake is today. Back then, NVIDIA had 1,500 employees and was growing fast. Now it has 17,000 employees and $12 billion in annual revenue. "This is why I wanted to come to Snowflake. I wanted to repeat the journey I took at NVIDIA," says Sunny.

The two companies were very different in another way, though. Founded in 1993, NVIDIA was started at a time when most tech companies used the client-server computing model. Its personal computers were connected to powerful server computers that it owned and operated. Cloud computing did not yet exist.

Starting about a decade ago, most technology startups have been born "cloud native," meaning all their serious data processing is done in the cloud. Snowflake was one of those. In the early days, one of the engineering managers, Jonathan Claybaugh, handled IT in addition to his engineering responsibilities. Recalls co-founder Thierry Cruanes: "We were using Software-as-a-Service products to keep the organization as lean and mean as possible." Today, all the major software applications the company uses run in the cloud, including Workday for managing business processes and Salesforce for customer relationship management.

By the way, NVIDIA is in the midst of testing Snowflake's cloud data platform for its own internal use. Sunny has switched teams, but a proof-of-concept project he launched there is continuing.

Sunny had been on the job for only a few weeks when he spoke for this book, but already he had sketched out a strategy for remaking Snowflake's IT organization. When he arrived, IT people were embedded within the major functional organizations. He pulled them together. At the same time, he continued or launched major initiatives in finance, sales, and engineering. The über-goal: laying the IT groundwork so Snowflake can run super-efficiently even while it continues to grow at a rapid pace.

SNOWHOUSE FOR FINANCE

Snowflake was on track to become a publicly traded company, so it was using its own technology platform to get its financial systems in order. At the company's annual sales kickoff event in Las Vegas in February 2020, Frank told 1,000 people in the audience that Wall Street analysts would want the company to be able to accurately guide on revenue growth, operating margins, and gross margins. "When we're ready, we'll go from playing on Saturday to playing on Sunday," Frank said, referring to the contrast between college football and professional football. The crowd roared its approval.

When it comes to analyzing financial performance, Snowflake has a significant advantage over on-premises technology providers. It has the ability to peer inside the system and see how, and how much, each customer is using the service down to the machine second. How many tables of data are they storing? What types of queries are they running? How many computer clusters do they use for different types of queries? How are things changing? The company uses this information to make the system faster, more efficient, and less expensive—but also to help forecast its financial performance.

At the same time, Snowflake is a consumption-based business, which creates forecasting challenges. Customers pay for what they use. Their usage can vary widely month to month or even day to day. Customers themselves often do not know how much they will use and when at the beginning of a time period.

This is where Snowhouse comes in. In addition to the customer usage data, Snowhouse contains all of Snowflake's billing data records of its consumption of cloud services from Amazon, Microsoft, and Google, along with other information that helps the company track revenues and costs. For instance, the finance department analyzes the data in Snowhouse to map out usage patterns for each individual customer, then rolls them all up to produce overall usage patterns. Snowflake uses machine-learning algorithms on the current and historical data to produce forecasts of future usage, revenues, and costs—which can be used to predict profit margins.

SNOWHOUSE FOR SALES AND MARKETING

Chris Degnan, the first sales person Snowflake hired and now the company's chief revenue officer, began using the company's data warehouse when he was a sales force of one. Today, practically everybody on the sales team employs it every day. Sales reps can see how their customers are using the technology, then, based on customers' needs, the reps recommend other uses for it. If a potential customer questions the system's ability to handle their most demanding data processing tasks, a Snowflake sales rep can query the system to see if another customer is using it in a similar way. How much data do they plan on storing? How many queries do they plan on running concurrently? How many data consumers will be hitting the system on any given day? The facts are at their fingertips in Snowhouse. The answer is almost invariably "Yes, we can," and with proof to back up the claim.

The Big Data revolution has transformed the practice of marketing. Practically every digital interaction between a company and a customer is trackable. When you stream all that data into a cloud data platform, you get a constantly evolving 360-degree view of each customer. Snowflake's marketing team uses its deep knowledge of customers and their needs to decide on everything from which e-book to publish next to who to invite to the next Data for Breakfast marketing event. That's a series of events staged across the world in which Snowflake and its technology partners explain how things work to developers, analysts, and business managers.

The field marketing team studies the results of past events to design and plan the next ones. How many people attended? What roles did they have in their companies? How many leads were generated? Which contacts translated later into sales? No longer is the marketing team operating based on impressions and instincts; they know what works. Because new information is constantly flowing into the data platform, they do not have to wait until an event series is over to see how it performed. They can modify their planning and redesign the events on the fly to get better outcomes.

Next up for Snowflake's marketing department: setting up a program within the company's new data exchange for sharing data with advertising and marketing partners.

SNOWHOUSE FOR ENGINEERING

In the old days of software, engineering teams tended to plan and prioritize the next updates of their products based on a little feedback from customers, a lot of guesswork, and the personal preferences of the engineering managers. When they were done coding, they "threw the product over the wall" for the field sales teams to catch and sell. For large and complex software products like databases, an upgrade might be delivered only every three to four years. This approach produced monolithic software products that were too often off target and out of date by the time customers installed them.

Today, in the cloud, Snowflake engineering teams make continuous improvements to their software. In addition, because they can see how customers are using them, they get immediate and actionable feedback. Much less guesswork required.

Snowflake feeds information about how customers are using the product into Snowhouse. In addition, it collects feedback from its customer-support system. The engineering team can look at this data and see which programming languages customers are using to construct queries and which kinds of queries return results quicker than others. Are customers using a new feature heavily, or do they try it and then stop? If customers are migrating from on-premises computing systems to Snowflake, the company's engineers want to see where problems emerge. They still ask customers what new features or improvements they want to see, but they do not have to wait for humans to answer. The feedback is in the data.

Snowflake's engineering team studies customer usage data to improve the way it operates its service day to day. Engineers review query execution telemetry data to improve the performance of queries, which lowers costs for customers.

The company has to anticipate demand and allocate resources among the underlying cloud operators, Amazon, Microsoft, and Google so computing resources are available, even when demand spikes. It's an automated process. Customers want to be able to launch data-processing tasks instantly. Snowflake's engineering team uses machine-learning algorithms to model and forecast usage patterns so it can have the optimal amount of computing power reserved and ready to go—not too much, which affects margins, and not too little, which affects customer satisfaction.

Snowflake also gathers aggregated data to create insights about usage so it can help customers use the Snowflake platform more effectively. By understanding how customers are using the platform at a granular level, it can help advise them on better ways to use it. It also knows the most effective ways for getting particular tasks done on the system, so if a particular customer is operating suboptimally, Snowflake can guide it to methods that would be more efficient. It's good for the customer, but it's also good for Snowflake, since it pays the cloud service providers based on usage, too. The ultimate goal is to remove impediments—including costs—that would deter customers from maximizing their use of the platform.

NEW TASKS FOR SNOWHOUSE

As this book was going to press, Sunny and colleagues within Snowflake's functional departments were working on a system for combining data from diverse sources to improve the way Snowflake bills customers. Until now, the company used software products provided by others. Now they are embedding the work in Snowhouse.

The heart of the new approach is a bespoke usage-metering system. Customers acquire usage credits in advance. As they use the credits, Snowflake bills them. Since some computing tasks are completed in a matter of seconds, the company needs a fine-grained system for calculating usage precisely—and a way of showing customers that get exactly what they pay for. The metering system also connects to Snowflake's Salesforce customer relationship management software and to its Workday financial software, but the invoicing itself takes place in Snowhouse.

Sunny also plans on using Snowhouse to manage IT operations. All the monitoring systems for data governance and cyber-security will flow into the data platform. Any security vulnerabilities or compliance issues can be spotted using pattern-recognition technologies—and can be immediately remediated.

"Everything we execute inside the company has to flow through Snowhouse," Sunny says. "It should be the *de facto* in how we talk and make all the right decisions in the company."

PART 2

HOW THE DATA CLOUD TRANSFORMS BUSINESS AND SOCIETY

5

THE DATA ECONOMY
AND THE DIGITAL ENTERPRISE

THE IDEA that data is the "new oil" went from a revelation to something of a cliché in a few short years, so the natural impulse is to drop the phrase and move on. But it's still a useful metaphor for a major shift in business and the economy, perhaps on par with the Industrial Revolution.

"It's not a perfect analogy because data isn't a commodity. Processing data involves both science and art," says Frank Slootman. "But the comparison works in other ways. Oil is energy. Everything runs on energy. Businesses are increasingly running entirely on data."

So it's fair to say that just as oil drove economic progress in the twentieth century, data is driving progress today. On one hand, that's because there is so much of it—like a West Texas gusher. Just as important, though, technological advances are driving progress, enabling people to transform data into insights and insights into actions that help businesses to thrive and the economy to grow.

The combination of so much data with the new tools for analyzing it gives rise to the Data Economy. That's an ecosystem where businesses, governments, social enterprises, and individuals succeed or fail based in large part on their ability to extract value from data. It's also a network where organizations and people share data and collaborate in ways that improve outcomes for all.

A digital enterprise is an organization that aggressively digitizes all its data; puts data at the center of its strategies, operations, and culture; and in the case of some routine processes, is literally driven by data instead of humans. It is a fundamental building block of the Data Economy. The Data Cloud provides energy for the Data Economy.

The idea that society and an economy could be powered by information is anything but new. In fact, the Mongols in the thirteenth century used census data to help manage an empire that stretched 4,500 miles from Kiev to Korea—counting not just people but animals and possessions.

Information technology has rapidly expanded the gathering of data. The electromechanical Hollerith machine powered the 1890 census in the United States. The IBM 077 Collator was essential to the development of America's Social Security system in the 1930s. The so-called Information Age got its start in 1959 with the invention of the MOS transistor at Bell Labs and flourished with the emergence of the personal computer. Then there was the New Economy, which grew out of the explosion of all things Internet in the 1990s.

What's different today is the sheer volume, variety, and velocity of the data that's available combined with breakthrough advances in digital networks, computers, and software. We had the big concepts back then but not the scale and speed of computing to act on them that we have today. Taken together, these developments make it possible to understand how the world works—the causes and effects of things—on a much deeper level.

The world's data is exponentially more valuable today than it was a few decades ago. That's not only because we have more of it. New technologies enable us to gather it faster than ever and to integrate different types of data to create insights based on models that simulate the dynamics of the physical world and mimic the functioning of our brains. Our computers provide insights at the critical moments when we make important decisions in our professional and personal lives.

Data analytics gives organizations and people digital superpowers.

You get a form of X-ray vision. For instance, consider a complex business problem such as how to best organize inventory in a brick-and-mortar warehouse and how to best select, pack, and ship it. Using advanced technologies, you gather a blizzard of data from sensors, inventory records, sales transactions, and other sources. You create a computer model of the warehousing process, run simulations to see which variations produce the best results, and refine the model. Then you get more data and repeat. Data enables you to closely examine and evaluate every aspect of a business process so you can improve it.

You also get ESP—the ability to peer into the future. Don't wait until you discover that your computer systems have been hacked and your most valuable secrets have been stolen. Get out ahead of the cyber criminals and spies. Use data analytics to probe your network for vulnerabilities, compare your setup with active attacks, predict what might happen to you, and patch things before you become a victim. Thanks to modern data analytics, you do not need to hire a team of consultants to probe your system. You can do it with software.

Surprisingly, given all the potential benefits, progress toward a full-blown Data Economy has been slower than many people expected. For one thing, earlier, most organizations did not have access to the proper technology tools to get the full benefit of all the data that is being created and collected. Thanks to the cloud, we can scale up our efforts to capture, process, and draw insights from all that data. At the same time, the performance of our data analytics engines has improved to the point where we can derive insights in seconds, not hours and days. All this has changed in the past decade, but it takes time for organizations and attitudes to catch up with the new technologies and possibilities. The technology is well ahead of our ability to use it.

Meanwhile, work remains to be done on the policy side of building the Data Economy. Unfortunately, we have all witnessed the downside of the world's fixation on data. Most notably, the political consulting firm Cambridge Analytica exploited Facebook's technologies to collect data from 87 million people profiles, most of them without explicit permission.

Because of the potential for abuse, policymakers, along with some of the makers and users of technology, are advocating for agreement on legal and ethical standards. The goal is to safeguard the rights of individuals, to protect their privacy, and to limit the way information about them is used by businesses and governments. Also, there is concern about protecting individuals from data-fueled manipulations that deprive them of agency. The idea is that only when rules are made and safeguards are put in place will data truly deliver on its promise as a force for good in the world used for the benefit of all.

CONTROLLING THE DATA GUSHER

The world's supply of digitized data has exploded over the past few decades. When IBM engineers designed the first commercial hard disk drive, which was released in 1956, it was nearly the size of a Volkswagen Beetle and had a storage capacity of just 5 megabytes. That's about as much as a couple high-resolution photos you have saved on your iPhone.

Today, there are about 50 zettabytes of digital data in the world, up from 2.7 zettabytes in 2012, and tech market research firm IDC forecasts it's going to top 175 zettabytes in 2025. (A zettabyte is

1,000,000,000,000,000,000,000 bytes of data.) According to IDC's calculations, it would take one person 1.8 billion years to download the data available in 2025.

Why so much and so fast?

For starters, the physics of computing has enabled businesses and other organizations to digitize and store information more affordably—with the prices of basic computing and storage plunging steadily over the years. But the gush of data in recent years has three primary causes. One is the expansion of the Internet. This is well understood. No reason to dwell on it here. The other main factors are advances in data types, which are produced by instrumentation and the biological sciences. It is worthwhile spending a little time considering them, partly because they are beginning to intersect in surprising and powerful ways.

Think of them as macro and micro.

On the macro level, the world is becoming "instrumented." This is the Internet of Things (IoT). Tiny sensors are being attached to everything from oil pipelines to your car to the watch on your wrist. These sensors capture images and measure all sorts of physical, electrical, and chemical attributes and activities. Wireless or wired networks collect the data, which is typically stored in disk drives stacked on racks in data centers. Estimates of how many sensors are now connected to the Internet range from 20 billion to 50 billion. By taking the measure of the world in this way, we can understand what is happening and how things work with more certainty and in a timelier manner.

Thanks to these IoT technologies, your family SUV can park itself and automatically apply the brakes when a jaywalker crosses your path. But even more consequential uses of the technology are on the way. Imagine this scenario: You live in south Florida. A hurricane is approaching. City leaders in Miami want to track the storm's path and forecast the damage it might cause, down to the block level, so they can plan for the worst-case scenario and react to whatever happens. Data collected about weather, tides, rainfall, traffic, utility outages, downed trees and calls to

911—much of it from sensors—can help civic leaders protect lives and property.

Today, this kind of information is available, but in most cases it is not collected in one place. To have maximum impact, it should be combined and integrated so it can be analyzed—and so police, emergency medics, and utility workers can be deployed most effectively.

Now, for what's going on at the micro level—in bioscience.

Each human genome contains about 3 billion DNA base pairs, and each human's DNA stores about 700 megabytes of data—the same as about a half hour of high-definition video. The first sequencing of a human genome took a decade to complete and cost about $1 billion. Today, technicians using $1 million machines can sequence a genome in a day at a cost of a few hundred dollars. In the future, gene sequencing will be as routine as pregnancy tests. It will be so fast and cheap that in advanced economies we will collect and store everybody's genome.

By studying an individual's genome, physicians can spot gene variants that might signal the risk of a disease. Frequently, several genes are involved. Those mutations, combined with stresses and environmental factors, can trigger the onset of disease. Also, researchers are now able to tell which drug therapies are likely to be more successful for a particular patient based on their genetic road map. It seems likely that someday scientists will be able to use gene editing technologies to repair faulty genes before they can cause trouble.

Today, institutions have begun to set up vast computer systems for storing and accessing genetic data, for research and for use in diagnosis and treatment. One of the great data gathering projects in history has just begun.

Now, take a look at how the Internet of Things and the genome are converging.

Let's use the scenario of a neonatal intensive care unit (NICU) in a hospital. An infant lies in an incubator hooked up to sensing devices for testing and monitoring her vital signs. If something goes wrong, caregivers will be alerted instantly. In addition, all that data from the sensors can be collected and analyzed.

Separately, the baby's physicians have access to her genetic data and her electronic health record—information about tests, clinical observations, diagnostic evidence, therapies, and treatment outcomes. Using data management systems, a healthcare organization can store, integrate, and analyze all of this information.

A number of large healthcare providers are doing just that—assembling computing systems designed to enable them to practice truly personalized medicine. They are bringing data from many of their existing computing systems into a centralized location where the information can be readily managed and analyzed.

In the not-too-distant future, it's likely that powerful artificial intelligence software programs will be attached to these vast data conglomerations. The AI will learn from every bit of information that streams into storage from IoT devices, from every medical image captured, from every genome sequenced, and from every word or click that a caregiver puts into a computer interface. They will be able to use insights from this process to improve diagnoses and treatments for individuals and for humanity as a whole.

This real-time melding of data and analytics will be able to deliver a personalized cocktail of care for one tiny girl in the NICU—and everybody else.

But for this scenario to be realized, healthcare systems will need a massive amount of digital storage and computation, much more than is available today using traditional computing technologies.

The same is true for all sorts of enterprises. They may not have data demands on the scale of a healthcare system, but because of the volume and diversity of data these days, many organizations face data management challenges that dwarf those they faced in the not-too-distant past.

A NEW WAY TO THINK ABOUT DATA

To deal with these challenges and with the opportunities created by data, business and government leaders are embracing the notion of building data-driven enterprises. They're developing strategies that put data at the center of their organizations so it drives all decision making.

If you are contemplating such a strategy, you might begin by taking an inventory of data. Consider the stuff you create yourself, the data you can obtain from business partners, data available for purchase, and potential new sources that you might not have contemplated yet.

It helps to think about data being in four concentric circles within and around an organization.

The first data circle runs along the boundaries of your enterprise. It's the stuff you collect from sales, inventories, customer interactions, tracking of operations, and the like. Typically, this data is collected by functional organizations and business units, and it is closely guarded by them. They would prefer that nobody else touched it. These are known as data silos.

The second circle contains data that is owned by business partners and can be shared. These are typically supply-chain or distribution partnerships, or marketing partners. Your organization and theirs are willing to share information when it is mutually beneficial. Often, however, the traditional mechanisms for sharing data make it difficult—costly and slow. A lot of data loses value over time, which can lead to low productivity and to errors in judgment.

A third ring is data available for purchase. Some companies collect and sell data as their core business—the Nielsens of the world. Other companies have discovered that data they produce in the course of doing business is valuable for others, and they sell it. Selling data has been a great business for some data providers; think FactSet and all its financial markets data. FactSet sells data via Snowflake's data exchange, but, too often, for other sellers and buyers of data, the mechanisms they use are too rigid and the costs are burdensome.

The fourth ring is still emerging. It's data that has not been collected yet, either because it has been too hard to collect or, until now, people saw little value in it. Think about what could be achieved by fleets of drones flying across the millions of acres of farmland in the middle of the United States. They could gather photographic evidence and weather data that could help farmers understand what's going on in their fields. Armed with this information, farmers can adjust right down to the individual row of crops the inputs they use to maximize yields. They might also be able to find out what crops have already been planted by other farmers so they can make planting decisions that will bring the best prices.

The same goes for other industries. For instance, drone or satellite images could be used to count how many cars are parked outside tech companies in Silicon Valley on Saturday mornings. That intelligence, along with many other inputs, could be used by investment strategists to assess how dedicated the employees of a particular company are to growing revenues and meeting the needs of customers. Are they 9-to-5 people, or are they so driven to succeed that they go to work on weekends?

All this data is out there, or it could be. In many cases, it's waiting to be unleashed. That's where a new generation of data management and analytics technologies comes in.

NEW TECHNOLOGIES FOR MINING DATA

All the data in the world isn't much good unless you can find it, access it, combine it, and analyze it. Today, way too much information is trapped in the sludge of outdated ideas and outmoded computer systems.

In many cases, data that companies already own cannot be used to full advantage because it is squirreled away in silos that are controlled by departments or business units. Many companies have tried to address this by consolidating their data in centralized data management systems running in their own data centers. But that is not really a solution. Often there are multiple copies of the same database, and all too frequently the contents of the "copies" do not match. Another problem is that different kinds of data cannot be readily integrated with one another.

When enterprises *are* able to get their data centrally managed and integrated, they encounter limited computing capacity. They do not have the computers and storage devices to handle all the data they need and all the analytics they want to do. At times of peak demand, business analysts might wait hours before they get to launch their queries, or wait hours for their queries to finish running. One option is to spend a ton of money on new hardware, but IT leaders shudder when they contemplate asking management to spend millions of dollars on equipment. It's not uncommon these days for them to have to ask for a 50 percent increase in capacity. That's per year. Then, assuming they get the O.K., much of their computing power sits idle during periods of less-than-peak demand. That's inefficient for the company and for the economy.

When organizations want to share data with partners, they run into problems, too—both costs and delays. Typically, the owner of the data uses a network protocol called File Transfer Protocol to transfer data. The organization uploads its data to an FTP site. The receiver of the data logs in to the site, authenticates, and begins the download. The process can take a long time, especially with today's file sizes. In some cases, it makes more sense to load the data onto a flash storage device and ship it by truck.

The solution to these problems can be expressed in two words: cloud computing. Only by moving storage and computation to the cloud can organizations begin to take full advantage of their data.

Public clouds—the kinds operated by Amazon, Microsoft, and Google—are elastic. They provide essentially unlimited storage capacity and computing power. These clouds are in reality collections of vast data centers that are distributed around the world and connected to the Internet via fiber-optic networks. They use standardized computer equipment and software, which makes them easy to manage. They are multi-tenant systems, meaning customers share resources. That makes them highly efficient and relatively inexpensive to run. Companies that use public clouds for their core computing needs do not have to buy and maintain server computers and storage devices. Amazon, Microsoft, and Google do that for them.

Today, enterprises are rapidly moving data from their traditional storage systems to the cloud. IDC forecasts that by 2025 about 50 percent of the world's stored data will reside in public clouds. Goldman Sachs predicts that 43 percent of all corporate computing will be done in the cloud in 2023. Large enterprises and tech startups are leading the rush, but it seems likely that the bakery down the street and your local credit union will eventually do the same.

When Hover first launched, it was a small company with a Big Data challenge. The plan was to use technology originally developed for use by the U.S. military to help transform the home improvement industry. The company, now a Snowflake customer, built a product that turns smartphone photos into accurate and customizable 3D models of the exterior of any home. Hover provides homeowners, insurance adjusters, and contractors highly accurate measurements to enable quick estimates. Its ability to produce 3D renderings of designs enables people to view and modify the potential results of remodeling jobs. Hover applies machine learning and computer vision to build the 3D models. The company could not exist without cloud computing.

But just moving your data to the cloud does not make yours a data-driven company. The data must be curated, transformed into usable formats, managed, secured, and made readily accessible to end users in your organization.

This is the work of a cloud data warehouse and a cloud data platform.

A cloud data warehouse is a highly controlled environment. It's where data is managed and made accessible. The data warehouse is transparent, it's secure, and it's connectable to the other technologies that you need to analyze data.

SnapTravel makes booking a hotel quick and easy using natural language processing and personalization technologies. The company's AI-powered technology searches the Web for the best available deals and collects all the information in Snowflake's cloud data warehouse. The company also gathers data from partners such as advertising agencies and social media platforms. With such a diverse array of data sources and types, it's essential to be able to put all of the data in a single warehouse, integrate it there, and provide access for all the business users in the company. That gives them one version of the truth, which is especially valuable in the rapidly changing travel business.

There has been a move by enterprises to store all their data in "data lakes," either in their computer systems or in the cloud. But a data lake is too much like a real lake: murky. It is hard to see what is in it and hard to hook the pieces of the data that you want. Think of a cloud data warehouse as a very large aquarium. It does the job of a data lake, the storing of all types of data, but it does it in a way that makes the data more easily accessible.

The cloud data platform is the technology ecosystem that includes and surrounds a data warehouse. Technologies associated with the platform make it easier to ingest data—to curate it, transform it into formats that are usable, and integrate diverse types of data with each other. Once the data warehouse is set up, a wide variety of technologies connected to the data platform can help organizations draw insights from data. These include business intelligence tools and dashboards for viewing and monitoring data, programs for measuring operational efficiencies, and computer programming and querying tools that enterprises can mix and match to customize their data analysis capabilities.

These are the essential technologies for the data economy. Without the cloud, cloud data warehouses, and cloud data platforms, companies that aim to be data driven are likely to experience frustration and, potentially, flat-out failure.

On the other hand, companies large and small that embrace these technologies have an opportunity to gather data and gain maximum value from it just like the big boys of the Data Economy—Google, Facebook, and Amazon. True, most companies will never be able to collect data on the scale of these giants, but cloud data technologies level the playing field, at least in terms of technology. Even more significantly, an organization that masters the acquisition and analysis of data positions itself to claim a sustainable competitive position within its industry. You do not have to have as much data as Google to be the best sushi restaurant chain in Illinois or the best professional baseball team on the West Coast, but your chances for success will improve if you are data driven.

THE ROLE OF THE INDIVIDUAL IN THE DATA-DRIVEN ENTERPRISE

While technology is critical for organizations that are on a path to data mastery, this journey also requires new thinking about the role of the individual in the organization. You have to make sure that everybody is participating, from the data scientist at headquarters to the sales assistant in the branch office in Peoria.

The job title "data scientist" is all the rage. These people are to the data-driven enterprise what the College of Cardinals is to the Vatican. They work largely out of sight, using arcane objects and rituals (Python, Scala, and machine learning). Every now and then a puff of smoke comes out of the chimney (a new simulation model or regression analysis algorithm).

Seriously, data scientists play a critical role in managing massive amounts of data and interrogating it to produce insights that can dramatically improve the performance of a business or government agency. That's because they possess the domain knowledge and the technology tools that enable enterprises to deal with the deluge of raw data—and harvest valuable insights from it. For the digital enterprise, data scientists are more important than ever before.

Before the rise of the cloud, enterprises typically employed armies of database administrators to set up and manage traditional databases and the computers they ran on. Today, with the new paradigm created by the cloud data warehouse, far fewer DBAs are required, and their jobs are changing. They are becoming problem solvers and strategists rather than maintenance workers.

Back when, companies hired armies of business analysts to slice and dice the data for sales, marketing, finance, and other departments. Today, there is more work than ever for business analysts. The SQL query language is their go-to data analysis tool, but they also are using powerful data visualization tools such as Looker and Tableau. Thanks to technology, their work has far more impact.

The data scientist role is where some of the biggest changes are taking place. A few years ago, there were very few of them. They typically had PhDs in mathematics, and considerable expertise in statistics and computer science. Today, there are tens of thousands of them, and many more are needed. Typically, a PhD is no longer necessary, but they still possess those cross-disciplinary skills.

Today's data scientists use a handful of modern programming languages, including R, Python, and Scala to write sophisticated analytical procedures, which often incorporate machine-learning algorithms. Their work is exploratory, and the goal is to be predictive. With machine learning, they don't necessarily have to know what they are looking for, specifically; they can turn their algorithms loose on the data to find patterns and anomalies that they did not anticipate.

While data analysis is becoming ever more sophisticated, there is also a move to put simpler—but still powerful—tools in the hands of people throughout an organization. We're talking about people like procurement specialists, warehouse supervisors, and even retail store managers, not the traditional dedicated business analyst. At one of Snowflake's customers, Office Depot, more than 6,000 employees routinely tap into the data warehouse. That includes managers and field sales people, and even warehouse workers and store clerks.

This phenomenon is called the "democratization of data," and its practitioners are sometimes called "citizen data scientists." In response to the imperative to make data more accessible and interpretable for additional types of employees, technology companies are developing a generation of tools that mask the complexity of data analytics from the end users.

DataRobot, one of Snowflake's technology partners, has taken the simplicity imperative to an extreme. Its platform enables regular people in a company—not just the experts—to describe in simple terms the problem they want to solve. Then the software chooses the best fit from a variety of AI tools and algorithms. After that, the system runs the analytical process and delivers the result in easy-to-understand words and numbers. It's automated AI for the enterprise.

Here's a fresh way to think about the need to make data insights accessible: Data analytics in the Big Data era is like a mountain covered in trees that gets a lot of snow in winter. It's an ideal spot for a ski resort. The resort developer is responsible for transforming a wilderness into a winter playground. It cuts down trees to make slopes and paths, builds lift systems, installs snow-making equipment, installs lights, and grooms the slopes after a snowfall. In any enterprise, data is the snow, employees are the skiers, and executives are the resort managers charged with getting people safely to the bottom of the slopes.

Another piece of advice for companies that are on the data journey: Measure everything.

Once you have placed your data in the cloud, and you are managing it with a cloud data warehouse and analyzing it, you need to devise a set of processes for carrying out your data strategy and metrics for measuring your performance. Remember, you are asking your employees to play by new rules and to acquire new skills—and to think differently. Metrics drive behavioral changes. And metrics produce more data, which you can then use to study, model, and optimize your use of data. This is the essential feedback loop for the digital enterprise in the twenty-first century—the flywheel of a data-driven enterprise.

For an enterprise to be truly data driven and to participate fully in the Data Economy, everybody who works there has to be data driven. You have to make sure they're all in your loop.

6

THE POWER OF DATA
NETWORK EFFECTS

N EARLY 2020, after it became clear that an outbreak of the deadly COVID-19 coronavirus that started in China could become a pandemic, governments, medical scientists, and healthcare institutions worldwide began marshaling their resources in response. One of the essential weapons in their arsenal was data.

Medical researchers in China, the United States, and other countries began sharing data so they could quickly create vaccines that would protect people from being sickened or killed by the virus. Meanwhile, scientists began gathering data to monitor the spread of the disease and predict how and where it would go next. At the Network Science Institute at Northeastern University, analysts used data from the U.S. Census, transportation networks, and health organizations to predict the spread of coronavirus based on the interconnections of its human hosts. They shared their models with policymakers.

Drawing data from numerous sources, a team of data scientists at Johns Hopkins University published a visualization showing the spread of the disease globally in real time.

Starschema, a technology services company, picked up some of the same data Johns Hopkins used, melded it with other datasets, and made the entire collection available on Snowflake's public data exchange in its COVID-19 incidence dataset. Within days, hundreds of organizations—including government agencies, healthcare systems, and public health researchers—were accessing the data.

Businesses could use the data to help them develop contingency planning and analyze supply chains for possible vulnerabilities. Public health authorities could investigate to determine, for instance, which strains of SARS-CoV-2, the virus that causes the COVID-19 disease, carry a higher risk. Governments could use real-time information about the spread of the disease to plan their responses. "Everyone is dealing with the effects of COVID-19 in one way or another. Our goal is to deliver data that is of the highest quality with the utmost transparency," says Starschema CTO Tamas Foldi.

Across the globe in the early months of 2020, organizations of all types began to rely on the gathering and sharing of large, diverse datasets as they collaborated to deal with the global health crisis. The only hope for an effective pan-societal response to the virus depended on this kind of cooperation and sharing of data.

This response to the coronavirus illustrates the power of data network effects.

Data network effects are the compounding benefits achieved by sharing data: combining diverse types of data from a variety of sources and making it available to others—one to one, one to many, or many to many.

Data network effects are cousins of network effects—the phenomenon that has reshaped communications and business with the rise of the

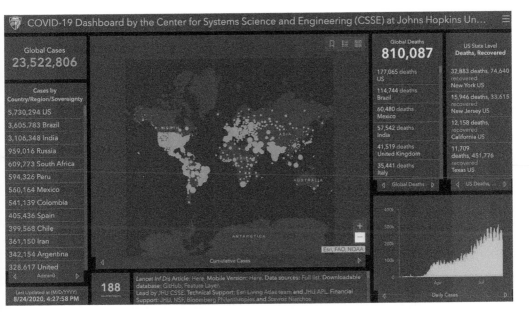

SOURCE: CENTER FOR SYSTEMS SCIENCE AND ENGINEERING, JOHNS HOPKINS UNIVERSITY

Internet. A network effect is the impact that each additional user of a product or service has on the total value created for the people and organizations it touches. Apple's smartphone app ecosystem and Facebook's social networks are examples of network effects at their most potent.

The Data Economy is powered by data network effects. The more data that is shared and the more individuals and organizations it is shared with, the more value is created for everybody involved. It seems likely that the organizations that master data sharing—and reap the rich rewards of data network effects—will be the Apples and Facebooks of the next wave of business innovation.

SLOWING THE FLOW OF DATA

There's a problem, though. Traditional computing paradigms sharply limit the potential of data network effects by constraining our ability to share data.

Although it is easy enough to share spreadsheets and datasets from traditional relational databases via email or other methods, the rise of Big Data overwhelms these methods, especially when the sharing crosses corporate or government boundaries.

One of the most common traditional methods for sharing large amounts of data between organizations is uploading it to a server computer that uses the File Transfer Protocol (FTP), a networking protocol designed to manage secure transfers of data between computers. The protocol has been in use since 1971. Such transfers tend to be frustratingly slow. In addition, after the recipients get the data they still have to transform it into usable formats to get any value out of it. That means more delays. Also, since the data is transferred in batches, it can quickly become stale.

A more modern option is using Application Programming Interfaces (APIs) to enable others to access data from your applications or databases. The sharer and user of the data have to write software code that enables the user to call functions that access certain datasets and pull results into their applications. It's like a college student calling home and asking the parents to put money into the checking account. That is not a great method for transferring large amounts of data, as usually each "call" is limited to a small number of resulting data rows. Plus, it's typically a one-way communication.

In both scenarios, copies are made of the data. That means the data is stored twice or many times, which has a cost. It also means that the copies will likely become out of date and out of sync with the original data. In addition, data governance—the rules that are established to control who gets to see the data and how it can be used—might be compromised. And the more copies, the higher the chances that a copy gets lost, altered, misdirected, or stolen.

THE DATA CLOUD MAKES SHARING EASIER

Cloud computing changes this game, making data sharing much easier. That's mainly because the public cloud, with its multi-tenant architecture, provides easy access to secure slices of data for an unlimited number of data consumers simultaneously.

In addition, cloud data warehouse technology addresses data sharing even more directly. Here's how it works in Snowflake's data platform: At the outset, Snowflake's founders made the decision to separate storage from computing. That makes it easy for anybody with a Snowflake account—and even those who are not Snowflake customers—to gain access to data that's stored in another account in the data warehouse, but only if granted these permissions by the owner of the data. To do this, the owner of the data sets up a "share" by specifying a set of database objects that she or he is willing to share with others. That package could include whole tables of data, or "secure views"—which are subsets of a table's rows or columns. At that time or later, the owner specifies the identities of others they are willing to share those objects with.

For instance, retailers might want to share their inventories in real time with one or more suppliers so they can automatically replenish products before the supplies run out.

When the consumers of the data gain access to it, they effectively are given a pointer, sort of like a hyperlink on the Web, to that data. They do not make a copy of the data, though. Instead, they create a "virtual database" in their Snowflake account that points to the actual data in the owner's account. Through this virtual database, they can begin querying the data or they can combine this new data with data they own themselves or got from other data providers. They do not have to go through the process of moving the data and reformatting it before they can use it. It just seems to magically appear.

This approach is highly secure. The data never leaves the Snowflake platform, nor does it even leave the Snowflake account of the data's owner. Think of it this way: You and your brother just checked into a hotel. Your brother is in the room next to yours. The two rooms are connected, but you have to unlock the door on your side to let your brother in, and he has to unlock his door to let you in.

There are a slew of other benefits to this type of data sharing.

Since there's no copying, the organizations involved do not have to pay for storing their own copies of the data, and they do not have to worry about the data being out of date or incorrect. There is one version of the truth.

With this setup, it's easy to control who gets access to the data and how they use it. If you want to stop sharing with a partner, you revoke their access and they are immediately cut off.

Another consideration: On Snowflake's drawing boards is a feature that will enable anybody who shares data in this way to run reports tracking who accessed their data, when they did it, and exactly which objects they accessed. Using that information, sellers of data, for instance, could modify their offerings and pricing based on shifts in demand.

Snowflake calls these sharing relationships "edges." That's a computer science term describing a relationship between two entities in a network.

Cloud data warehouses make possible nearly friction-free data sharing. Snowflake's leaders believe that a mass migration of computing to the cloud is going to be essential for maximizing data network effects, and that cloud data platform technology, in particular, will grease the skids for sharing.

People who do not have regular Snowflake accounts can share on an ad hoc basis, using a so-called reader account. But the real value comes when organizations establish deep, long-term, strategic sharing relationships with one another. That happens when all parties involved have their own Snowflake accounts. Sharing is faster and easier. Data consumers can set up an edge and forget about it—and, bingo, fresh data just shows up. Data sharers can push a button and share with anyone, anywhere in the world. There's unlimited concurrency, too, meaning no matter how many people are querying the same data, it won't slow down response times. "It's like a million people being able to borrow the same book from the library at the same time," says Justin Langseth, vice president for Snowflake Data Exchange.

Think of Snowflake as the YouTube for data sharing.

For each of Snowflake's more than 3,000 customers, the fact that all those other organizations are storing their data in Snowflake makes the cloud data warehouse even more valuable. They can easily share data with one another. By sharing data, they can improve their situational awareness and forecasting. If two customers are already business partners, they can collaborate more effectively and develop deeper levels of data-backed trust. Also, every other Snowflake customer becomes a potential customer or partner. When two Snowflake customers forge new B2B commerce or partner relationships, they can immediately begin sharing data in both directions.

EXPEDIA GROUP SHOWS HOW IT'S DONE

Expedia Group isn't just Expedia.com, the big online travel agency. It is actually made up of more than seventeen brands in the travel space. Some of the brands are well known—including Travelocity, Orbitz, Hotels.com, VRBO, Trivago, HotWire, and Cheap Tickets. The company also "white labels" its services for hundreds of partners in the travel, hospitality, and banking businesses.

Most of the brands began their lives as independent companies before being purchased by Expedia Group. After the purchases, they continued to operate semi-independently. But now the group is busy integrating the operations—and the data—of its many brands. "The goal is to operate as a unified travel platform," says Aaron Davis, senior director of data intelligence. "That way, we can offer a different value proposition. We understand the domain of travel, we know our customers, and this gives us the ability to offer them the kinds of experiences that they will enjoy."

Aaron plays a key technology leadership role in understanding and improving Expedia Group's conversations with customers—whether on the phone, on websites, on smartphone apps, via email, or through social media.

The newest element of the conversation management platform is the use of virtual agents equipped with natural language understanding technologies to conduct conversations with travelers and the company's business partners. The virtual agents are capable of handling initial contacts with people and of suggesting the next-best action a human agent should take when assisting travelers or partners. There are more than 500 million conversations handled annually per year spanning all the brands in Expedia Group.

The goal: to gather all the conversation data, put it in Snowflake's cloud data platform, so analysts and systems can learn from all that input rather than being limited to just the data pertaining to their slice of the business. Already some of the brands are operating this way, with more data integration and sharing to come.

One of the use cases is for business analysts at the brands to be able to tap into the data platform to spot patterns and trends so they can improve interactions with customers. For instance, they might be able to improve the handoff from the automated agent to a human one—so it's done at the most effective point in a conversation. Perhaps the virtual agent, using sentiment analysis of the words and phrases the customer uses, detects that the individual is becoming frustrated. Time for the switchover.

The data platform also enables the company to respond to changes in travel conditions on the fly. For instance, if the company is alerted by an airline that a flight has been canceled, it can reach out to people who were supposed to be on the flight to offer them other options. Based on their records of interactions with that customer, they'll know what communications method would be most welcome—say a text, an email, or a phone call.

Expedia Group is developing capabilities that will enable it to respond to the need for multiple, last-minute changes in travel plans. Say a hurricane has suddenly shifted course and is heading for a vacation hot spot. Expedia Group wants to be able to quickly come up with alternate itineraries for customers that might involve several of its brands. The company will be able to assemble offers based on customers' travel histories and then reach out to them via communications channels that they are most likely to respond to. The company will be able to seamlessly shift from one communications channel to another as needed, consolidating all the information about the earlier conversations. That way, customers won't have to repeat basic information about themselves and their travel plans each time they start a phone call or Web chat with an Expedia Group agent.

Being able to react this way requires Expedia Group to be able to pinpoint data signals in near real-time from systems inside or outside the company and use machine-learning algorithms to place that information in context and make it immediately usable.

USE CASES FOR DATA SHARING

Snowflake has identified a handful of typical models for sharing data. Justin calls these "sharesonas"—riffing on the way consumer marketing firms create personas to segment markets. In each case, the cloud and sharing capabilities like those Snowflake offers are essential building blocks.

THE SILO BUSTER: Expedia Group fits in this category. Departments and business units within a large enterprise typically collect data for their own use and stash it in their own databases. Those are data silos. A cloud data warehouse makes it easy for those parts of an enterprise to share data with one another. Frequently, separate organizations within an enterprise set up Snowflake accounts and begin storing data there—then they discover that sister organizations have done the same. It's a cinch to open doors between them so they can begin sharing more robustly.

THE CONNECTED ENTERPRISE: Every business has an ecosystem of suppliers, partners, customers, and others that it cooperates with to get things done. The outsourcing trend has made such linkages even more important. With open communications and coordination, these ecosystems can operate like virtual enterprises. Cloud data sharing can make them even more nimble and responsive. Sharing between enterprises is easier, faster, and more secure. By providing real-time data transparency to business partners, enterprises can deepen relationships, build trust, and collaborate with others more effectively.

An example is Rakuten Rewards, which runs the largest consumer loyalty program in the United States. Shoppers earn cash back for purchasing from participating merchants. Rakuten Rewards uses data sharing within the Snowflake cloud data platform to allow outside firms to analyze its data. That way, the company can get input from people with advanced expertise for special projects, without having to hire high-priced experts for a temporary need. Rakuten Rewards is also a silo buster in its own right, using data sharing within the larger Rakuten company to dramatically enhance the power of the Rakuten Rewards datasets.

DATA AS A SERVICE: The market for data has been booming with the recognition that enterprises can deepen their understanding of their markets and shift economic trends by combining third-party data with their own. A growing number of companies are in the business of selling, consolidating, brokering, syndicating and enriching data. A cloud data warehouse enables these companies to share data with customers in a more granular and secure way.

Some advertising technology firms provide the whole array of digital advertising services for clients—including troves of data that helps them identify and reach consumers. These companies also typically provide analytics services and advice to help clients use the data to plan and manage campaigns and measure their performance.

THE DATA SUPER-CONSUMER: Enterprises in a number of industries, especially financial services and consumer packaged goods, have become ravenous users of data from third-party sources. They want context. Rather than shopping externally for data and importing it into their databases the old-fashioned (and inefficient) way, they set up private cloud data exchanges and invite their data providers to interact with them there. The buyer calls the shots.

Say a hedge fund purchases information from thousands of sources. In the past, it had to set up separate sharing relationships and processes with each of them. It was a nightmare. Now the firm is asking its data providers to interact via a cloud data exchange. Once the system is set up, data will flow quickly with a minimum of oversight.

THE COALITION: There are situations in business and society where the problems we are confronted with extend far beyond what single enterprise and its business partners can manage. One example is banks dealing with the cybersecurity challenges they all face. If they pooled all the data they gather about malicious exploits, they would be quicker to spot vulnerabilities and new threats. They would be better equipped to fight off a common enemy. Or think about a major metropolitan airport. What if all the airlines, airport management, the Federal Aviation Administration, and the local transportation authority shared data about the flow of people in and out of the airport? They could all plan better and collaborate to improve operations and reduce the public's frustrations with air travel.

SAAS SHARING: Software-as-a-Service companies store their customers' data in the cloud. But in many cases, each customer's data is kept in a silo. Using a cloud data warehouse for data sharing, SaaS companies can more easily provide real-time data analytics as a service to their customers. They can integrate their own data with that of their customers to provide broader insights. And they can aggregate data from multiple customers in an anonymized fashion that enables customers to compare their performance in the marketplace with that of their peers.

A great example is Braze, a marketing engagement platform that delivers orchestrated customer experiences across a wide array of communications channels—including push, email, texts, smartphone apps, and more. Behind the messaging is a sophisticated data management and data analytics system built on Snowflake's cloud data platform. Every interaction and transaction with every end customer is stored in the cloud. Braze analyzes its customers' data to evaluate the effectiveness of campaigns in real time so they can quickly be modified. "We want our brands to deliver messaging that's friendly, relevant, contextual, and timely, and ultimately is going to strengthen relationships with customers," says Jon Hyman, the company's co-founder and CTO.

In earlier days, Braze transmitted all the engagement data out to its customers for them to do anything they wanted with it. Now, for customers that have Snowflake accounts, Braze streams the interaction data it collects on their behalf into Snowflake and shares it with them in real time. That way, all the data is in one place, it does not have to be manipulated before it can be used, and any number of business analysts and data scientists can query the same data at the same time.

As additional companies start using this approach to data sharing, more "sharesonas" will emerge. Some of them might be quite surprising. For instance, when the fintech company Square sold off a food delivery subsidiary in 2019, it found that data sharing eased the handoff of the business. This came as a bit of a surprise, since the data associated with the subsidiary's business was mixed in with Square's in its Snowflake cloud data platform. How would they separate the data and transfer it? But it turned out they did not have to. The acquirer was already using Snowflake. On the day the deal closed, Square simply created an edge and shared the relevant data with the acquirer. Then Square handed over ownership of the data. Under other circumstances, it might have taken months to disentangle the subsidiary from Square. Instead, it took one day.

That's another display of the power of data network effects.

7

DATA EXCHANGES

N THE WORLD of hedge funds, strategy and human judgment are essential—but data is also absolutely critical for helping a fund outperform its peers. Fund managers consume and analyze large, varied amounts of data, much of which is collected from the usual sources. However, they also use data feeds that supply them with financial information about individual companies, markets, and economic conditions. So how does a fund distinguish itself?

For Coatue Management, a technology-focused investment manager based in New York, the answer can partly be attributed to its use of a variety of alternative sources. For example, the fund uses datasets to better understand trends of certain industry segments and companies in addition to building a more complete picture of the broader investment environment.

You have heard of "black swans." Those are events that are nearly impossible to predict and have a potential for producing severe consequences. The folks at Coatue hope their data acquisition and analysis will help them spot key trends that their competitors miss.

Going forward, Coatue expects Snowflake's technology to play a key role in its data strategy. It is beginning to use Snowflake's data exchange technology to operate its own data management platform. Instead of handling hundreds of data feeds separately, the firm plans on migrating many over to the exchange and consolidating them in a single cloud data warehouse, where it will be easier to manage and make available for analysis.

"At Coatue, we understand the role data plays in smart investing and we aim to be at the leading edge of data management," says Thomas Laffont, co-founder and senior managing director. "The exchange eliminates traditional data boundaries and enables real-time, frictionless data sharing that will yield key benefits for our ongoing data investments."

Using the data exchange, Coatue will be able to better evaluate the quality and value of data provided by third-party suppliers. It will also allow the firm to increase the speed at which it forges relationships with original data generators in order to support its continued quantitative analysis efforts. While fundamental research has been at the core of Coatue's strategy since day one, its focus on utilizing software and data analytics to make investment decisions has grown significantly over the past few years.

Some of the magic of the data exchange is that companies no longer have to rely on established data aggregators to provide them with the data it needs to perform at the top of its game. Some of those aggregators have virtual monopolies on certain types of data, and they charge princely sums for access. Now, thanks to the exchange, if a firm chooses, it can begin to forge direct relationships with the originators of the data it needs. It can get the data it wants faster, and for a better price. You can envision how this "unbundling" can help unleash data and transform the way data is bought, sold, and shared.

We've talked about the key elements of Snowflake's cloud data plat-form—the data pipeline, the data warehouse, the sharing technologies, and the support for dashboards and analytical tools. All those capabili-ties are important, but if there's a "killer app" on the platform (and there is), it's the data exchange. The exchange is where all the capabilities come together with the potential to help companies become truly data driven and to grease the skids for commerce and collaboration between groups of companies—potentially for entire industries.

"We are starting to have the network effect of more and more custom-ers connecting with one another, and we're becoming that data network," says Matt Glickman, vice president for Snowflake Data Marketplace and customer product strategy.

TWO KINDS OF EXCHANGES

Snowflake has two exchanges, public and private.

The public exchange, called the Snowflake Data Marketplace, is a free-to-join marketplace that enables Snowflake customers to acquire data from third-party providers—or anybody who has data to sell—so they can easily discover, access, and generate insights from it. Customers are able to connect with the exchange through their Snowflake accounts and browse a catalog of datasets that they can add via the sharing feature to their existing data on Snowflake. All Snowflake customers can see all the items in the catalog. Customers do not incur any storage fees related to the data they access via the exchange.

For data providers, it's a new business model. Rather than market-ing and selling their data only from their own websites or other owned channels, they can list their products within a shared marketplace and gain access to Snowflake's more than 3,000 customers. Data providers can make their products available to all or to specific customers. There's no copying or sending files, and all datasets are up to date. At this point, the financial transactions take place on the data providers' websites, but in the future, Snowflake will support transactions within the exchanges themselves.

The folks at Snowflake first came up with the idea of the public exchange. They saw it as an App Store for data. But after discussions with a handful of customers, they realized that a private exchange might have even more appeal.

The private exchange enables organizations to create their own branded private version of a data marketplace. This is what Coatue uses. The "owners" of these exchanges have complete control over which assets are listed and who has access to them. The private exchange provides access to third-party data sources chosen by its owner—including those available in the public exchange catalog. In addition, the private exchange enables the owner to access data from business partners and other sources that are not broadly available. The owners of these exchanges control who sees what and decide what data others get access to and when they get it.

Exchange owners and data providers are able to monitor activities on the exchanges that they are involved with. They can use activity metrics to help them understand who is using what and which data is most valuable.

The private exchange has a catalog, too. But instead of showing every participant the entire universe of datasets, organizations or individuals see just the ones that are available to them. It's like getting an L.L. Bean catalog that includes only clothes that fit you.

There will be a variety of ways that organizations use these exchanges. Coatue's is one avenue, while Wunderman Thompson Data's is another. Using the exchange, Wunderman Thompson Data is able to enhance the customer experience, making its data assets available to customers in a deeper and richer way than it would be able to provide via a public data marketplace. Data buyers, like Coatue, and data providers, like Wunderman Thompson Data, both are able to use the private exchange to optimize their business objectives.

Enterprises might choose to set up an internal private exchange specifically to make it easier for their own business units to share data with one another. No buying and selling. Retailers with huge and complex supply chains might shift the management of their data-sharing relationships with those suppliers to a private exchange. Public health organizations might set up a private data exchange to share data and collaborate to deal with a global health emergency, such as the coronavirus. Again, no money changes hands.

You can imagine an enterprise setting up a private data exchange so it provides a view into all its business activities, internal and external. Think of it as a data supply chain. All those business activities have data associated with them. Employees, based on their roles in the enterprise, can gain access to all the data they need to do their jobs through their personal view into the organization's private exchange. It's a mix of company-owned data, public exchange data, and private exchange data, and it provides them with a data-centric view of their world.

The exchange is the doorway to the digital enterprise. It's a marketplace—potentially, the Amazon.com for data. It's also a data network. And when a large number of organizations use it, you have a data economy operating on Snowflake's cloud data platform.

THE CONCEPT OF "DATA TONE"

To fully appreciate the potential power of the data exchange, we have to travel back to the time of Alexander Graham Bell. In 1876, when Bell called a colleague for the first time using a device we now call the telephone, it was the beginning of a revolution in communications. Anybody could connect and communicate with anybody else by simply picking up a device and dialing or listening.

A key feature of telephony that helped it scale ultimately to billions of users was the dial tone, which came along early in the twentieth century.

That's a signal sent by a public telephone exchange or a private branch exchange (PBX) to a telephone indicating that the exchange is working and is ready for them to call someone.

At first, telephone exchanges were handled manually by operators who physically connected one terminal device to another on a network by moving plugs on a board. Later the exchanges became automated. They managed the dial tone and made the connections without human intervention. These innovations created massive network effects, where the more people are on the network, the more useful and valuable it becomes.

You can see where this is going. In the data world, the analogue for dial tone is data tone. The data tone makes it easy for anybody's data to be easily combined with anybody else's data, and for a person or a computing system to have a "conversation" with the data. By mixing the data in sophisticated ways, the data engineers, who are responsible for preparing data, enable data scientists and other analysts to query it and derive insights.

The data exchanges, public and private, are the Bell Telephones and PBXs of the data universe. Before the exchanges, parties sharing data had to manually connect to one another so the data could flow. It was painful. The exchanges automatically enable not just one-to-one connections but also "data conference calls" in which many organizations share data. The exchange catalogs are comparable to yesterday's Yellow Pages.

Look into the future, and you can see that exchanges and data tone could help enable a massive amount of data commerce. Start with commerce between the traditional sellers and buyers of data. In addition, enterprises could monetize the data they collect in the course of doing business—selling slices that might have value to other companies. It's even possible that *individuals* could begin selling data on exchanges in a secure and privacy-protected way. Brands and retailers are desperate to get to know who you are and what you want to buy, so make them pay for the information.

DATA SUPPLIERS AND DATA MONETIZATION

The business of selling information has been around for decades. Think Nielsen, LexisNexis, the credit reporting agencies, and the Bloomberg terminals. Exchanges change the game for data sellers. Now they can market their goods in a virtual shopping mall, easily make connections with buyers, and share data with them.

The exchange offers Wunderman Thompson Data an opportunity to radically transform the way it does business. "The data marketplace and the data sharing opportunity are some of our core focuses for the future," says Adam Woods, Wunderman Thompson Data's chief technology officer. "It's a better way to integrate and share."

Historically, Wunderman Thompson Data used a conventional data management system running via its own data center, to manage their AmeriLINK consumer database. From there, the company switched to a cloud-based data warehouse offered by one of Snowflake's competitors. The service, however, proved difficult to manage and was unable to keep up with the high demands of data analytics, especially during peak seasons and shopping periods.

Having worked in those former data management environments, Adam describes the exchange as being nothing short of "transformative" for business. Wunderman Thompson Data is now able to operate in a highly secure and compliant environment, while managing its interactions with customers more fluidly. By shifting the AmeriLINK database to Snowflake's exchange, the data is more easily discoverable and shareable, and readily accessible for customers. Additionally, Snowflake breaks down traditional data boundaries by eliminating the need to change hands via APIs or the more primitive forms of data transfer (as described in Chapter 6).

Another key feature of the exchange for Wunderman Thompson Data is the ability to understand exactly how clients are interacting within the AmeriLINK database. For example, identifying which datasets are used more frequently and how valuable they are to clients. With these tracking insights, Wunderman Thompson Data can optimize value and price accordingly.

Other data suppliers are flocking to Snowflake's exchanges. Weather Source, for instance, provides historical and real-time weather data to customers so they can create business intelligence around logistics, footfall traffic, financial analysis, and more. DemystData offers its massive repository of 500-plus data products, including data from well-known providers such as Acxiom, Experian, and Infogroup. Another major data seller on the exchanges is FactSet, which collects, normalizes, and manages financial markets and corporate financial data for thousands of subscribers. Bryan Lenker, vice president and director of client and technology solutions, says a lot of work typically goes into setting up subscriptions for clients, but a data exchange changes the game. "We can go from days down to minutes," he says. "This is an extreme accelerator across all facets of business."

Another component of the data exchanges is a new generation of data services. In the past few years a large number of data technology specialists have emerged that focus on managing and analyzing data for specific industries or business functions. They offer value-added data integration and transformation services. Consumers of data will be able to find those service providers in the data exchange catalog with the ease of performing a Google search.

TRANSFORMING INDUSTRIES WITH DATA

Because of the private exchange's ability to enable sharing of data easily and securely in one-to-many, many-to-one, and many-to-many modes, you can see how it can support collaborations within a single company's supply or distribution chains—or across an entire industry. Think about the uses of blockchain for securely sharing information and recording transactions on a private network. Some of that work could be done on a cloud data exchange, and with much less technological complexity and organizational angst. In other scenarios, a cloud data exchange could be complementary to blockchain.

Blackboard, the education technology software giant, has just this sort of cross-industry data-sharing initiative in mind. The company has begun establishing a private data exchange serving the needs of its entire universe of education customers plus data providers and other participants in the education ecosystem. In this way, not only can an individual institution get the convenience and security of a data exchange; all of the participants in the ecosystem can share knowledge that cuts across the industry—potentially improving the quality of education.

"Our clients have embraced this concept of centralization of data in order to improve the insights that they can derive from it," says Jay White, Blackboard's vice president for software engineering. "By pulling data together from institutions willing to share their data, we can help derive insights that just aren't possible from the myopic view of a single institution's data."

Blackboard launched its cloud data platform for sharing data with clients last July, initially enlisting 200 institutions. Early in 2020, it began outfitting its private exchange. Overall, the company has more than 16,000 clients in 90-plus countries serving more than 100 million students, so there is a lot of potential for collaboration on the exchange.

Last year, Blackboard collaborated with ACT (the testing organization), the University of Maryland Baltimore County, and others in a research project that in part used data gathered from its cloud data platform. It was a study of the relationships between students' social and emotional maturity and their performance in an online course. This example shows the kind of insights that could be gained from industry-wide collaborations and data sharing that Blackboard hopes will take place on the new data exchange.

Blackboard has begun loading thought leadership materials onto the exchange. The first such piece was an online course designed to help the learning analytics community use Blackboard's rich dataset.

Institutions of higher education—which are one of Blackboard's main focuses—are under intense pressure these days. Among small private colleges, the economic environment is downright hostile: Enrollment is dwindling, deficits are soaring, and more closures are likely on the way. Public colleges and universities face challenges, as well. State funding is declining for many of them, and graduates face huge debt loads. Even elite universities are not immune. They have to figure out how to deliver more effective and relevant programs without spiking tuition. "The institutions that are going to survive and thrive are the ones that are making the smartest decisions, and those decisions are driven by data," says Jay.

Two issues are front and center for higher-ed leaders: how to personalize courses and coursework for individual students, and how to spot students who are struggling so they can help them before they fail or drop out. These are the kinds of issues that Blackboard helps schools confront using its cloud data platform.

Richer datasets and more collaboration between institutions promise to help address these issues and more—improving the effectiveness of pedagogy and improving students' quality of experience on campus and online. "We hope to help drive a collective wave of innovation and learning that we in education haven't seen in a long time," says Jay.

Other data and data analytics providers are exploring ways they can use the data exchange to serve the common good. For instance, Braze, a customer engagement platform for consumer brands, has begun experimenting with the data exchange. For starters, it has begun posting benchmark data from trillions of marketing interactions with consumers for any Snowflake customer to use—for free. Brands can use the data to evaluate metrics such as email open rates and advertising click-through rates from their marketing campaigns. They can compare their performance against other companies in their industry or across industries.

The data is statistically valid, since the dataset Braze shares is from 600 brands in the United States and European Union. It gets updated weekly.

A MARKETPLACE FOR DATA

The impulse to create a marketplace is as old as human civilization. As soon as there is more than one person in a place, the conditions exist for exchanging something of value for something else of value—whether it's a stone tool traded for an animal hide in prehistoric Africa or nutmeg traded for cinnamon in fifteenth century Venice.

Technology has played a key role in making modern marketplaces work, including stock exchanges and Amazon.com. Technology companies have attempted to create online marketplaces to facilitate commerce between companies. Remember the dot-com boom? Several companies developed such marketplaces. One of them, Commerce One, formed an online marketplace called Covisint with General Motors, Ford, Daimler, Renault, and Nissan. Ultimately, amid the dot-com bust, it came to nothing.

Here we go again. The idea now is to create new kinds of marketplaces for information, to facilitate the trading of dollars for data. There is general agreement that data has tremendous value. It could decide the fates of companies and countries in the coming century. So, marketplaces for data—that's really a no-brainer.

Will Snowflake's exchange model work? It seems to have some built-in advantages. The sharing mechanism in Snowflake's technology is vastly superior to preexisting alternatives—making it easier to share information in a secure, quick, and efficient manner. Potential participants are already there, thousands of them with Snowflake accounts, congregating in the virtual town square. Flip a switch, and they are trading in the marketplace. Participants do not have to take a risky plunge. They can ease in with baby steps. The public and private exchanges are up and running. A few dozen companies have joined, and more are coming every month.

Think about the beginnings of the New York Stock Exchange. In the years after America's Revolutionary War, traders bought and sold stocks and bonds on the cobblestones of Broad Street before eventually moving indoors. There wasn't much to trade in those days—mostly war bonds and a few bank stocks. Compare that to today's financial markets: the immense value of daily trading, the colossal market cap value of all of the publicly traded companies combined, and the dizzying array of trading entities and vehicles. We have come a long way.

Will data marketplaces follow a similar trajectory? Will people some-day be trading data futures? Will certain kinds of data become commod-ities? Hard to say. But it's clear even now that the data marketplace is a very big idea. It's potentially a game changer not just for Snowflake and its customers and for the operators and participants in other exchanges, but ultimately for capitalism and the global economy.

8

DATA GOVERNANCE

THE BATTLE between businesses and the forces that aim to invade, corrupt, cripple, spy on, and steal from their computer systems is a constant game of one-upmanship. For every new barrier or monitoring system that organizations erect to protect themselves, hackers, thieves, spies, and fraudsters develop new tricks for getting around them. It seems like the world is stuck with an endless cybersecurity arms race.

But every now and then an idea comes along that offers hope that the good guys may at last gain a sustainable advantage. Hunters, a tiny Israeli startup, has just such an idea. Hunters is harnessing artificial intelligence to provide proactive threat detection. It's a data-driven security approach built for the Data Cloud.

This kind of work is normally done manually by teams of security consultants. But that is costly and likely to miss clues that machine-learning algorithms can catch. The promise of Hunters' automated solution, Hunters.AI, is that it can spot evidence of impending or active cyberattacks better than humans and can alert target organizations before traditional cybersecurity systems will.

Conventional cybersecurity software packages tend to focus on just one piece of the security puzzle—networks, email, Web, personal computers, or smartphones. Hunters.AI gathers data and security telemetry from all those systems, manages it within its customer's account on the Snowflake cloud data platform, and uses AI to spot anomalies. The company's founders, Uri May and Tomer Kazaz, based their solution on deep knowledge of malicious tactics and techniques they learned while serving in the Israeli military's famed 8200 Unit, which is known for its cybersecurity expertise.

When a security breach occurs, evidence of it is scattered all over the place, but the traces are hard to find. Hunters.AI is trained to detect those weak signals and connect the dots between them. "We're using AI to scale these sophisticated, nuanced tasks. Cloud technologies enable us to process massive amounts of data rapidly," says Uri, Hunters' CEO.

Hunters' scenario is just one facet of security in the cloud. In fact, the cloud creates a new paradigm for cybersecurity. Early in Snowflake's history, many large enterprises shied away from putting their data in the public cloud. They were afraid that the multi-tenant architecture meant it would be easier for malicious players to break in and steal or destroy their data. Yet reality has proved their fears to be overblown. When the proper measures are taken to secure data in the public cloud, the story changes. "We went to the extreme on security," says Benoit Dageville, one of Snowflake's founders. "Now a lot of customers are coming to the cloud and Snowflake because they see that security is actually better here."

Security is a component of a larger thought: data governance. With the rise of Big Data, social media, and artificial intelligence, data governance has emerged as an ever more critical issue for enterprises. It includes data cataloging and provenance, data security and privacy, regulatory compliance, and data quality. "Governance is top of mind for a lot of people," says Christian Kleinerman, senior vice president for product at Snowflake. "Companies have realized they need to use data more to build better products and services, and they have also realized how important it is to manage and protect their data."

Data governance is an essential piece of becoming a data-driven enterprise. It has to be designed into computer systems—not tacked on later. Data governance is designed into Snowflake's cloud data platform.

THE CLOUD CAN BE SAFER

Policymakers and the public began to focus on privacy in response to hacking and the harvesting of personal data by social media outlets. That's why we have seen regulations controlling the use of personal information. The European Union's General Data Protection Regulation governs the way personal data is protected and gives individuals control over how their personal information is used. California's Consumer Privacy Act, which went into effect on January 1, 2020, gives California residents the right to know what personal data about them is collected, to have a say in how it's used, and to request that a business delete any of their personal information it has collected. More national and state government regulations are sure to come.

To comply with regulations of this type—and to win and keep the trust of customers—organizations face higher-than-ever expectations concerning security, privacy, and governance. The good news is that, in spite of the early worries about the cloud, a cloud data platform like Snowflake's can actually be a better environment than traditional on-premises computers and databases for securing data and controlling the use of data.

There are several reasons for this.

But first, consider the weaknesses of traditional systems. Companies with conventional IT setups typically have data scattered in separate computing and storage systems—and in different physical locations, including different nations. That means they have a large number of points of vulnerability and situations that need to be managed and secured. They may have different rules for governing data in different locations. Managing all this is complex and expensive. Most companies other than industry giants can't afford to pay for the staffing and technologies to do so. And even among the industry giants, most security measures are reactive in nature. Many organizations don't know they have been hacked until the FBI knocks on their door.

The cloud and cloud data platforms turn this situation on its head.

When organizations commit their data to the cloud, they're sharing the responsibility for guarding their data with some of the most resourceful and security-conscious organizations in the world—Microsoft, Google, and Amazon. Many of the vulnerabilities in traditional computing environments exist because the systems haven't been configured properly, or the software hasn't been kept up to date, or the latest security patches haven't been applied. In the public clouds run by the big three, these vulnerabilities are largely dealt with by the cloud operators. Just as the famous Bubble Boy had his compromised immune system protected from germs by a plastic outfit, these clouds protect your data from malicious code with bubble-like policies and technologies.

In spite of these protections, vulnerabilities remain that the organizations storing data in the cloud must address. They have to put in place conventional security methods, such as firewalls and virus scanners, to protect the points of entry to their networks—laptops, smartphones, and other personal computing devices. They also need to set up and maintain authentication and permissions rules and procedures to prevent unauthorized people from accessing their data. Snowflake has these access protections built into its software by default.

Other important aspects of data governance are managed in a cloud data platform such as Snowflake's.

When an organization moves all its data to the platform, it gets rid of problems caused by having databases—and copies of them—scattered all over. The data is now cataloged and managed centrally. Copies can't be made and lost. Rules are established that cover all the data, and how it is stored and used.

Every piece of information is organized in tables, schemas, and databases, which ensures that it is fully governed by Snowflake's technology. This is especially important for the personal and company-confidential pieces. Additionally, tags can be created and associated with each piece of information, which helps with classification and search. That way, implementing governance policies is simplified. When an individual customer asks to be "forgotten"—for all the information about them to be erased—identifying the relevant pieces of data and deleting them becomes a much simpler process.

The metadata tags are useful not just for humans but also for machines. That's important in a world where, increasingly, routine processes are handled machine to machine, taking humans out of the loop. When an automated business process is initiated, the machines know what data they can use and how they can use it.

A cloud data platform makes it easier to share data securely. Think about some of the traditional methods for sharing data—faxing, emailing, burning it on a DVD, and dropping it in a mailbox, and uploading it to FTP sites or Web sharing sites. All those methods involve making copies of data and exposing it to risks. On a cloud data platform such as Snowflake's, when data is shared it is not copied and never leaves the safe confines of the data warehouse. A system for securely sharing data makes it easy and safe for organizations to show datasets to others in a fine-grained manner—and, if desired, to instantly revoke permission to see it.

Further, as we saw in the Hunters' scenario, a cloud data platform makes it easier to secure computers, networks, and data. It enables organizations to consolidate all the data related to security in one place. That way their security services can use machine-learning algorithms to spot anomalies and patterns across data types that might signal a vulnerability or an intrusion. And rather than just looking at traditional indicators of risk or infection, security systems can easily bring in other kinds of data. Was an employee just fired? Did they turn in their laptop, as required? Have all their computer access permissions been revoked?

You can also consider what's being chatted about on social media. If somebody makes threatening or hostile comments about the organization on Twitter, you can be alerted to it automatically, and your security service can evaluate the risk of cyber damage.

In these scenarios, typically, a customer shares all the datasets related to security with a third-party security service such as Hunters. Those services continuously search the data for clues. All this happens within the Snowflake cloud data platform.

This approach enables organizations to be more proactive in the way they deal with cyber threats. By taking advantage of sophisticated cloud data analytics, they can spot patterns that indicate not just intrusions but vulnerabilities. That enables organizations to get out ahead of the malicious actors—to plug holes before the bad guys can exploit them.

You can see that this is another situation where the power of network effects could come into play. The more customers share their security-related data with Hunters and companies like it, the more the AI systems learn about vulnerabilities, risks, and malicious exploits. The result would be that all the participants in the data network become more secure.

HOW TO PROTECT AND CONTROL DATA

You read in Chapter 4 how Snowflake uses an instance of its own technology, which it calls Snowhouse, to run much of its business. That includes data governance. Increasingly, Snowflake customers see the cloud data platform as a key piece of their security and privacy strategies—and they see analyzing data as an essential piece of securing their data. At the top of this chapter, Benoit talked about how Snowflake went "extreme" on security. The measures that Snowflake has taken could be seen as a checklist for any company contemplating moving its data to the cloud. Here they are:

ENCRYPT DATA IN TRANSIT AND AT REST: If an unauthorized person gains access to data, they must not be able to read it. That's where encryption comes in. The cloud data platform should protect data when it's moving through a network or at rest, stored on a disk. It's best to use the Advanced Encryption Standard (AES) with 256-bit keys.

KEY MANAGEMENT: Like practically everything else, encryption keys have a life cycle. Cloud data systems should be able to manage the generation, storage, distribution, use, and disposal of keys. For any data warehouse, you should limit the amount of data covered by an encryption key and the time the key is used. Critical elements are key rotation, a method for periodically generating a new key to protect newly ingested data; and rekeying, a method for re-encrypting previously stored data and disposing of old keys.

MULTI-FACTOR AUTHENTICATION: This is a double-check on the identity of a person seeking access to data in the cloud. After a person types in her username and password, she has to add a code that is sent to her via email, text, or phone call.

GOVERNMENT COMPLIANCE RULES: Organizations in industries that operate under government privacy regulations, such as healthcare and banking, should implement more advanced security features and policies designed for their industries. In addition, they should consider running their data warehouses inside a virtual private cloud, which is an isolated section within a public cloud.

Snowflake created a specialized version of its data warehouse, Virtual Private Snowflake (VPS), that is designed for organizations that want maximum isolation from other organizations' data and data processing tasks. With VPS, enterprises get a single-tenant instance of Snowflake within the cloud.

The VPS technology automatically encrypts all data at rest and in motion. It ensures customer control and data protection by combining a customer-provided encryption key in addition to a Snowflake-provided encryption key and Amazon Web Services user credentials. To keep unauthorized people out, the product supports multi-factor authentication, role-based access control, and IP white-listing—so only people whose IP addresses are trusted can gain access.

VPS is more expensive than conventional accounts, but for certain types of organizations it's a smart choice.

In Chapter 7, you read about the Snowflake Private Exchange. It's a data hub or marketplace that enables organizations to privately share data with a select group of trusted people or organizations. The private exchange provides enhanced security.

In contrast to the public exchange, these are walled gardens that are controlled by a single participant or, perhaps, by a group of affiliated organizations. In this scenario, outsiders don't even know the exchange exists—and they have no way of discovering it, much less seeing who is participating or what data they're sharing.

THE FUTURE OF DATA GOVERNANCE

In Chapter 3, you read about Snowflake's Black Diamond customer advisory retreat at a resort outside Scottsdale, Arizona, in early 2020. When members of the advisory board were invited to help set priorities for Snowflake by voting for topics that were of primary concern, many chose data governance.

The company has a wide range of features to help organizations govern their data with higher confidence and greater ease, and it is investing heavily to deliver new and improved capabilities. A key feature of Snowflake is called secure views. It enables the owner of a dataset to control who sees what on a granular level. Snowflake takes care in how it processes queries against the secure views to ensure there is no accidental leakage of security information.

A related new capability is the ability to establish dynamic data policies. Certain values in columns in databases can be exposed for some individuals but hidden from others. This is similar to what is enabled by secure views, but the policy is enforced dynamically, without having to create objects to specify the security policy. For instance, all but the last four digits of Social Security numbers and credit cards could be redacted. Or a person in France might be able to search only for data about people or events in their country.

Another area of focus is the support of policies based on data classifications. The system can take action or prevent operations based on tags associated with particular pieces of data. The goal is to ensure that data is used only according to policies or use cases it is intended for.

All these moves are designed to enable organizations to do ever more powerful analysis of data without the risk of violating privacy or secrecy rules.

Just like with cybersecurity, other aspects of data governance are in a state of flux as we migrate more data to the cloud. For each new problem or vulnerability that emerges, new rules and technologies will be needed. This requires a lot of care and vigilance, but the ability to take full advantage of the Data Cloud makes it all worthwhile.

9

MARKETING

THERE ARE many ways for consumer brands, retailers, and marketers to irritate people with whom they would like to forge close, lifelong relationships. Consider the four deadly sins of twenty-first century marketing:

SIN NO. 1: Not recognizing customers when you meet them. People call customer service and are forced to repeat their basic information, first for a robot and then for a succession of live service reps as they are passed from one to another in search of an answer to a simple question.

SIN NO. 2: Pitching customers products they bought weeks ago. A customer made the blunder of shopping online for undershorts. Now, every Web page he looks at serves up ads for undershorts.

SIN NO 3: Not knowing how individuals like to interact. A customer likes phone calls with real people. You offer her chats with bots.

SIN NO 4: Spam. Some marketers think it's smart to design email pitches so it's hard for recipients to block them. The result: Before you irritated them; now they hate you.

Today, many brands are guilty of committing some or all of these offenses. But there is no excuse for it. Modern marketing software, data management systems, and data analytics tools make it possible for brands to know who they are dealing with—no matter whether it's online, on the phone, or via a smartphone app. These new technologies enable brands to know a great deal about a customer's preferences and to know how they like to interact. And they know when their outreach falls on deaf ears, or, worse, alienates customers.

These capabilities are available in the Data Cloud. In the cloud, companies can gather all their data about customers in one place and easily cross-reference and match customer IDs. Because they store data in the cloud, they can track interactions as they move from one marketing channel to another. In the cloud, companies can ramp up or down their computing and storage capacity based on whether it's the night before Christmas or a lazy summertime afternoon.

One marketing services vendor that has mastered the Data Cloud is Braze. It offers consumer brands a robust marketing cloud service—built on Snowflake's cloud data platform—for managing interactions with their customers across all communications channels. According to Jon Hyman, co-founder and CTO, Braze is all about orchestrating customer experiences that are part of a continuum of interactions. In other words, it eliminates the four deadly sins. "Our focus is on helping to humanize the communications between brands and consumers on a global scale," Jon says.

THE DATA CLOUD FOR MARKETING

As Snowflake has expanded its footprint across a range of industries and geographies, the company has discovered that marketing is one of the horizontal applications that resonates most strongly with enterprises large and small. That's because the combination of digital marketing and cloud technologies make brand-to-customer communications more personal and targetable than ever before.

While there are many ways that enterprises use the Data Cloud for marketing, four have emerged as clear winners.

A 360 VIEW OF A CUSTOMER: This holistic understanding of consumers as individuals has been the Holy Grail of marketing professionals for decades. Now they can get it. A number of tech companies offer marketing clouds—Salesforce Customer 360 and Adobe Experience Cloud, for instance. These suites of integrated applications help enterprises profile customers and plan and orchestrate marketing campaigns to reach them. The profiles are created with customers' permission from loyalty programs and other data sources. Profile information and records of an individual's interactions with the brand—digital and physical—are captured and integrated with each other.

The data from marketing clouds is more useful when it is combined with other information that an enterprise collects or purchases. This is where a cloud data platform comes in. There, all the data can be easily combined, manipulated, and shared in a secure manner.

Say a brand is launching a product—a kitchen counter "safe" that holds cookies and kids' game controllers until they have finished their homework. The marketing team builds personae of the types of people they believe will most likely buy the product, mainly working moms with elementary-school kids. Then it matches those characteristics with real people in the profile database. Marketers might build a propensity model that enables them to rank customer segments from highest—meaning most likely to buy—to lowest. Then, based on records of past interactions, they can design a marketing campaign targeting likely customers with pitches that are most likely to appeal to them. This might be a combination of email, digital display ads, social media, and smart TV. Marketers can continually analyze the performance of marketing campaigns so they can refine them on the fly.

ATTRIBUTION: John Wanamaker, the American retailing and marketing pioneer, is credited with coining the phrase, "Half the money I spend on advertising is wasted; the trouble is, I don't know which half." Well, thanks to the new technology tools, advertising and marketing isn't a crapshoot anymore, or at least it doesn't have to be. In the past, the performance of marketing was measured by how many people were reached. Now it can be measured based on the response to those contacts or impressions. We can accurately measure the business return on investment of every marketing campaign and every dollar spent. This capability is called attribution.

"One of the biggest shifts in marketing is chief marketing officers are being measured on business outcomes, not just marketing performance," says Bill Stratton, who leads the Media, Entertainment, and Advertising vertical at Snowflake. "That means that they've got to tie their marketing activity to business outcomes as measured by data."

The customer 360 view is the starting point for attribution. How many of those moms responded to an email pitch or an ad on Facebook? Where did they complete their purchase? Did they later call the customer service line with a complaint? Once they bought the product, did the marketer stop pitching it to them? A cloud data platform enables marketers to easily combine their customer 360 and campaign data with corresponding information from sales and support. You know how much the campaign cost. Now you can figure out if it paid off. And you can use all that information to design better campaigns in the future.

THE "CLEAN ROOM": Because of new privacy regulations in Europe and California, many brands now handle personal information in more disciplined ways. They build detailed personal profiles when they get permission from individuals. However, in many cases, they are not allowed to gather additional information about those individuals from other third-party sources. That limits their ability to target ads accurately. For instance, if they don't know which of the people on Facebook are already their customers, they can't easily serve ads to them or to people who are like them.

Using "clean room" technology, however, marketers can select a set of customer profiles, redact identifying information, and match those now-anonymized profiles with segmentation information provided by a social media advertising platform. In this way, the marketer can target individuals who are most likely to buy their company's products without knowing who the individuals are. A cloud data platform not only provides this safe haven for customer profile data. It also can create a record that verifies no queries that involve sensitive personal information.

CAMPAIGN DATA FEEDBACK: You can see how technology enables brands to tap into a wide variety of information sources, integrate the data in the cloud, and use it to orchestrate more effective marketing campaigns. The campaigns themselves also produce a treasure trove of data, which can be captured and used to deepen understanding of customers and to better evaluate campaign techniques. Ad tech and analytics companies share that raw data back to their clients so they can use it to improve customer relationships.

HOW BRAZE SHARES MARKETING DATA

Braze provides granular marketing data feedback to customers. Its service is called Currents. Braze captures data about campaigns from its own systems and from email and push marketing partners. It streams the data as soon as it's captured to Snowflake's cloud data platform. It then shares the data with others, without the data ever moving. There, Braze, its clients, or analytics partners can look for patterns in the data or run specific queries on it. With its cloud data platform, Braze is sharing data continuously with its clients.

Earlier in its evolution, Braze fed back data in batches rather than continuously. That enabled clients to analyze events, such as a consumer abandoning a digital shopping cart on an e-commerce website. They could perform analysis to figure out why that happened. It's a useful exercise, but it's very backward looking. Data gets stale and loses value with the passage of time. It's better to stream data continuously. If you learn in real time that one of your customers has just abandoned a cart, you can send a push notification to their smartphone offering assistance. Continuous data sharing enables real-time interventions.

Braze got its start in 2011 with the name Appboy. In the early days, the focus was on improving engagement between smartphone app publishers and their customers. Back then, it was mostly one-way communication, from the app to the consumer. And typically, the messages weren't personal.

With time, the organization grew up and the founders changed the name to Braze. (Brazing is a method for joining pieces of metal.) The strategy matured, too. Braze now offers a platform to help marketers orchestrate consumer experiences and conversations across all channels.

A main focus is on collaboration. Even now, many companies have different teams for each marketing channel—a Web team, a mobile team, etc. Plus, they have business analysts and data scientists assigned to each of the campaigns. Often, people on the different teams don't communicate with one another, and they rarely share data. With Braze's technology, they can more easily collaborate on cross-channel orchestration, and, with Snowflake's cloud data platform, they can easily share and analyze data.

These days, Braze engages monthly with many millions of active users on behalf of its clients. It sends out billions of messages per day, including personalized emails, push notifications, and text messages. It looks for patterns in the records of trillions of discrete encounters spread out over weeks, months, or years.

Operating in the cloud is essential to Braze's success. And it's not just because of the ability to store and manage a huge quantity of data there. Braze typically uses up to 10,000 server computers per week. Being able to tap into immense cloud computing resources is critical. So is the elasticity of the cloud. The company's data scientists are constantly experimenting—trying new machine-learning techniques and testing hypotheses. They spin up servers quickly and test things out, then try something else.

The goal is improved customer satisfaction. "We want our brands to deliver messaging that's friendly, relevant, contextual, and timely," Jon says. "Ultimately, we want to strengthen those relationships and add value for the end consumer."

REAL-TIME RESPONSE

These days, companies need to see what's happening in the marketplace with real-time data. Marketers can change the course of interactions with customers on the fly or quickly modify marketing campaigns if they do not produce the desired results.

Electronic Arts, a global leader in digital interactive entertainment, uses the cloud data platform and analytics not only to orchestrate product launches but also to update the content of games if marketers spot opportunities to improve customer enjoyment. EA has dozens of game studios around the globe producing hit franchises in multiple languages.

The gaming industry is a hits-driven business, where companies are focused on fewer, bigger titles that hold customers' interest for a long time. The first few days and weeks after launch are critical. EA's publishing and sales people monitor sales patterns closely. A lot of the success or failure of a title depends on word of mouth, so EA listens to the global online conversation. Its people also monitor how players are interacting with online games. As a result, the publishers know what gamers are reacting positively to. They highlight those features in their marketing campaigns and promotions. They also add features, from new characters and vehicles to new game modes and multiplayer maps, depending on the game.

They can do all this because they have a continuous data feedback loop—which is made possible by their cloud data warehouse. Historically, it took as many as eleven days for planners in game publishing to see detailed sales data. "At times, we were flying blind," says Vlad Valeyev, chief architect of company operations. "Now we can make point-of-sale data register in the analytical product within minutes from the moment it becomes available."

Another benefit of keeping much of EA's global data in the cloud is that, in some situations, publishers and sales people can run queries not just across their studio's data but also by peeking over other studios' shoulders. That way, they can spot patterns and lessons that might improve their outcomes.

Sharing information is becoming essential for marketers, no matter what business they are in. In the old days, many business units and functions within an enterprise hoarded their data, or they shared it with others in ways that left the door open for outdated or incorrect information to infect decision making. With the Data Cloud, everybody knows what everybody else knows—and they know it immediately. Marketers can practice their craft with a precision and timeliness that was impossible before. Brands and customers are the ultimate winners.

10

MEDIA, ADVERTISING, AND ENTERTAINMENT

THE MEDIA, advertising, and entertainment industries have been undergoing major shifts in technology and consumer behavior for years. To get a sense of how much things have changed, compare the business landscape for these industries in the 1960s with conditions today.

In the 1960s, television was exploding. Families typically gathered around a single black-and-white picture tube, with just four or five channels to fight over. Today, there's a flat-screen TV in practically every room, and smartphones have become TV sets. There are thousands of "channels" to choose from.

In the '60s, every town in America had its own print newspaper, and many cities had more than one. Today, the newspaper industry is collapsing. Many towns have no newspaper. Last year, Newseum, the journalism museum in Washington, D.C., closed its doors.

In the '60s, giant movie palaces showed the latest Western or romantic comedy on panoramic screens and in vivid colors. A handful of studios decided what audiences wanted. Today, thousands of small, nimble studios produce motion pictures designed to appeal to a wide variety of audiences. Many go straight to TV.

In the '60s, creative geniuses on Madison Avenue pitched consumers TV ads for everything from Buicks to baked beans—based largely on their gut instincts. Today, the most productive advertising platforms are digital, and the iconic Mad Men are being elbowed aside by artificial intelligence.

In this era of rapid creative destruction, few industries have been creatively destroyed more than media, advertising, and entertainment. Many forces have been at work. Digitization, the Internet, smartphones, and social media are major disruptors. Different industry segments are being buffeted in different ways. It's not a simple story. But at the core, we are seeing two fundamental shifts: transitions from guesswork to knowledge and from mass communications to personalization.

For Bill Stratton, who leads the Media, Entertainment, and Advertising vertical at Snowflake, the critical importance of data for these industries hit home a few years ago when he was hired by a major TV network to assess the company's marketing strategy. After six months of research, he was asked to sum up his findings for a roomful of executives. "I'll give it to you in one sentence," he told them. "We think we know our audience. We have no idea who our consumer is."

The media, advertising, and entertainment industries could now be in for an even bigger transformation. Their use of data could bring more change in the coming decade than they have seen in the past half century. This shift is made possible by the Data Cloud and machine learning.

These three industries are linked by symbiotic relationships and by data. The Data Cloud unifies the entire media-advertising-entertainment value chain. By using a cloud data platform, participants can easily aggregate a wide variety of data from different sources, share data with industry partners, and control the use and movement of data to protect personal privacy.

The benefits of using a cloud data platform fall into three buckets:

UNDERSTAND YOUR CONTENT AND AUDIENCE: Media and entertainment companies can store, manage, and analyze all their consumer, advertising, and content consumption data to gain deeper insights about programming and audiences. This helps them deliver relevant, engaging experiences for consumers.

RESPOND TO CHANGING CONSUMER DEMANDS: Players in all three industries can make informed and timely decisions by tapping into a single, reliable, well-managed data source that's available to everybody at a moment's notice.

PROTECT PERSONAL PRIVACY: The ability to have one-on-one relationships with consumers comes with grave responsibilities. Using a cloud data platform, you can manage and securely share personal information internally and externally while obeying consumer privacy regulations. Cloud data platforms allow you to perform all the analytics, modeling, and segmentation without actually moving any consumer profiles.

Because brands and media and entertainment companies now have direct-to-consumer connections, they can develop private relationships with consumers that foster trust and transparency. These connections enable companies to see what the consumer is doing on a much more granular level so they can improve the customer experience and develop more relevant products and entertainment content. Says Bill: "This flywheel effect didn't exist before. It's utterly transforming the media, advertising, and entertainment industries."

DATA IS THE CURRENCY OF ADVERTISING

The story of Wunderman Thompson helps illustrate the massive changes that have come to the $565 billion global advertising industry. The firm was founded in 1958 as Wunderman and became the nation's first direct marketing firm. It was later rolled up into larger advertising organizations. Over the years, data collection and analytics became an essential piece of its business—which flourished with the rise of digital commerce. Last year, Wunderman acquired America's first advertising agency, J. Walter Thompson, which had been established in 1864. With this combination, the parent organization, WPP Group, melded two essential pieces of the advertising business: data and creativity. "We're able to work together in ways that just weren't possible before," says Adam Woods, chief data officer at Wunderman Thompson Data, the firm's data analytics unit.

Here's how the melding works: If a creative team is working on a multi-channel ad campaign (TV, mobile, search, social networks) on behalf of a brand client, they will want access to a wide variety of information about the brand, its customers, and how the brand engages with customers online, via mobile, and in physical stores or other in-person experiences. Since many brands now gather first-party consumer information through loyalty programs and other initiatives, the creative team will likely have access to a considerable amount of information about individual customers. In addition, the creative group will also have access to more generic consumer information, so-called third-party data, which helps them understand and address consumers who are not in loyalty programs. Wunderman Thompson Data provides the firm's creative teams with the data and the tools to harvest insights from both.

To help manage these relationships, the data unit has engaged with Snowflake. It stores and manages its data in the cloud data platform—and shares the data with creative teams and brands using the privacy-compliant data sharing features and the data exchange. (We described the firm's use of the data exchange in detail in Chapter 7.)

Having this kind of data platform is key to being able to discover not just the impressions created by advertising but the responses to it. Say you are a pickup truck manufacturer advertising on sports TV channels and websites. You want to know how many people went to a dealer showroom after they saw the ad, and how many of those people actually purchased the pickup, and, if they bought, how did the ad influence them. Armed with this kind of capability, the ad industry and its clients are finally able to connect the dots between ads and financial results.

This is just one slice of the advertising technology industry. Ad tech is an umbrella term that describes systems for serving up, analyzing, and managing advertising campaigns conducted on digital platforms. It's an ecosystem of companies and mechanisms that supports a highly automated two-way flow of information. On one end, you have the advertisers and the demand-side data and technology providers, such as Wunderman Thompson Data. In the middle, you have automated ad exchange platforms that manage real-time bidding for ad placements. On the other end you have the publishers (TV, Web, mobile) and their supply-side data and technology platforms. You can see how every player in such an ecosystem could benefit from putting all their data in one place in the cloud and sharing it flexibly with other participants.

AccordantMedia, another Snowflake customer, got its start as an independent trade desk for media exchange. But it shifted over to employ sophisticated data analysis and machine learning to track real-time bidding in the online advertising arena.

The company, which was acquired in 2016 by Dentsu, advises brands and agencies on ad bidding strategies—with the goal of not just getting the best deal on ad placements but also the best return for dollars spent. "We optimize every ad buy so you get more bang for your buck," says Balaji Rao, vice president for technology at Accordant Media.

CONTENT WAS KING. NOW DATA IS, TOO

In January 1996, Bill Gates, then the CEO of Microsoft, penned an essay arguing that in the coming Internet Era, content would be king. He wrote: "Content is where I expect much of the real money will be made on the Internet, just as it was in broadcasting. The television revolution that began half a century ago spawned a number of industries, including the manufacturing of TV sets, but the long-term winners were those who used the medium to deliver information and entertainment."

It turned out that handheld devices, analogues to the TV sets of yore, have more than held their own in the "real money" category, but even they have been overshadowed by platforms that aggregate bite-size pieces of information and entertainment, most prominently Facebook, Twitter, YouTube, and other social media platforms. They don't create content, but they do an amazing job of distributing it. This was a different sort of content revolution than Bill could have imagined.

Those distributors of content seem likely to continue their winning ways, and many companies will succeed (or fail) when operating in their shadows. But now that the Internet Era is giving way to the Cloud Era, the ready availability and power of data will help create a host of winners. Many will be in the media and entertainment industries, and thanks to the supremacy of data many will likely be in the content business.

That's because the Data Cloud—combined with advances in mobile communications and other fields—is helping to turn the content delivery world upside down. Remember, the cost of storage and computing in the cloud continues to go down as usage goes up. This factor, along with the on-demand nature of the cloud, allows companies and industries to connect, manage, and automate the sharing and use of data in ways never known before.

Look at Netflix, Amazon Prime, Hulu, and Disney Plus. More of the same is coming. These so-called over-the-top media services are streamed to viewers over high-speed Internet instead of through traditional distribution platforms. With the spread of high-capacity 5G wireless services, smartphones will become much more like TVs than they are today. The new content distribution technologies and methods not only put content owners in command; they also create direct relationships between them and consumers.

Content owners can use the data they gather from interactions with individual customers to make better recommendations to them and to create better content for them. Consumers get the content they want, when they want it, on whatever device they choose. For content providers, there is a flywheel effect. As their content becomes more relevant and compelling, customers become more loyal and more interactive, which solidifies the bonds between a brand and an individual—and throws off yet more data.

This data is collected in the cloud, where it can be structured and blended in ways that make it more available for analysis.

One of the key Data Cloud technologies for the media and entertainment industries is indexing. That includes the ability to deconstruct every piece of content into metadata tags that describe it so that information can be easily searchable and combinable. In parallel, you can index every interaction between the content owner or the piece of content and the individuals who consume it. We are talking about every movie, TV show, Web video, blog post, podcast, or meme. The content owner can use metadata for search—to get insights. But the owner can also use the metadata to make better recommendations to individual viewers.

An industry of data analytics software companies has emerged to help networks, production studios, cable TV companies, and others deal with the near-chaos of today's highly fragmented media and entertainment landscape. One of the players, RSG Media, has been in the game for thirty-five years but has shifted its technology to Snowflake's cloud data platform to provide the kind of scale and real-time response that its clients now require.

RSG Media manages content, marketing, and advertising inventories for its clients. In addition, it gathers the rushing stream of Nielsen viewership data and combines it with information from more than fifty other sources, curates the data for individual clients, and loads their slices into Snowflake for them. There, both RSG Media analysts and the clients' analysts go at it.

The company has an AI-based toolkit for analyzing data. It helps clients with predictive analytics—running "what if" schedule simulations to forecast audiences and help clients optimize their programming schedules. If clients are losing audiences, RSG Media helps them pinpoint why it's happening and identify strategies and tactics for reversing the trends. "This is a global market that's constantly on the move and evolving," says Shiv Sehgal, RSG Media's chief product officer. "Faced with increasingly complex challenges, media companies require new tools to assure they'll have strong positions in the future of television."

BETTER STEWARDSHIP OF DATA

With knowledge comes responsibility. That is becoming one of the core tenets of the era of the Data Cloud. As media and entertainment brands gather more information about individual consumers, it's on them to protect the privacy of those individuals and to manage the direct-to-consumer relationships in ways that do not violate their trust or even make people uncomfortable.

Adam, of Wunderman Thompson Data, says the disciplines of data governance and compliance have long been baked into his firm's business practices and processes. "We take these things seriously. We give the consumer the opportunity to opt out," he says. New data privacy rules in Europe and California mean that all businesses that collect personal data about individuals must adopt strict governance policies.

One of the critical features of a cloud data platform is its ability to manage data stewardship. The Data Cloud is great for gathering and blending data of all types—for knowing who customers are and what they want. The cloud data platform is built for governing that data.

On the cloud data platform, every piece of data comes with a metadata tag that describes who owns it, how it can be used, and how it can't be used. When data is shared, it is not copied. Rather, the organization that gets the "share" can see the data and use it for analysis, but it can't remove it, change it, or copy it. If a customer changes her mind about how their data can be viewed or used, that decision is instantly attached to the data. Or if she wants to be "forgotten" entirely, her information is deleted. Since it wasn't copied, one click on a keyboard is all it takes to restore privacy. If organizations share data that contains personal identifying information, they can create "clean rooms" where key bits of information are obscured.

The media, advertising, and entertainment industries have faced wave after wave of changes, and more are ahead. But thanks to the Data Cloud, companies in these industries can take much of the guesswork out of their businesses and forge direct relationships with their customers. The technology allows them to better understand their content and their audiences, and to respond quickly to consumer demands—without violating trust, the bedrock upon which all brands are built.

11

RETAIL AND CONSUMER PACKAGED GOODS

FOR TWO DECADES, Amazon.com has rocked the retail world—ever since founder and CEO Jeff Bezos vowed "to sell everything to everyone everywhere." With its online shopping, tremendous supply-chain efficiencies, low prices, and focus on customers, the company gut-punched one retail segment after another—first books, then gadgets, then clothing, toys, shoes, and discount department stores. Amazon seemed to threaten nearly everybody who owned a cash register.

And the pressure on traditional retailing is not abating. In 2019 alone, more than 9,300 brick-and-mortar locations were shuttered in the United States, an increase of more than 55 percent from the previous year. The global coronavirus pandemic has put additional stresses on the industry that could leave it in shambles.

Before the virus struck, though, a surprisingly large number of retailers had learned to successfully straddle the realms of physical and online selling. They were holding their own or even thriving in a rapidly changing, ultra-competitive world. The lessons they learned will likely be even more essential in the post-virus world.

One such retailer is J. Sainsbury PLC, which operates the second-largest chain of supermarkets in the United Kingdom. J. Sainsbury has more than 1,400 Sainsbury's supermarkets and convenience stores. It also runs the Argos chain of general merchandise stores and the Tu clothing brand. The first Sainsbury's grocery store was established in London in 1869, so this is an organization with staying power.

There are many factors in J. Sainsbury's resilience, but a key one is data.

The company recognizes the power of data to grow its business profitably, and it's using data management and analytics technologies aggressively and strategically—including Snowflake's data platform. Says, Helen Hunter, group chief data officer for J. Sainsbury. "Data is very important to Sainsbury's because one of the core tenets of our strategy is to put customers at the heart of everything we do. Our purpose is to help our customers live well for less, and we do this by offering them fair prices and great quality wherever and whenever they want."

MOVING DATA TO THE CLOUD

J. Sainsbury's example helps make the case that the demise of brick-and-mortar retailing is not inevitable. Retailers that offer consumers attractive propositions and convenience can not only survive but thrive.

Like J. Sainsbury, a number of other established retailers are doing well in part because they take full advantage of data to improve their revenues and profits.

For many, an important step was moving data to the cloud. The combination of a cloud data warehouse with powerful data transformation and analytics tools can help retailers save money in their IT budgets while empowering their data analysts to do more valuable work. The same goes for consumer packaged goods (CPG) companies and other consumer brands.

For most companies, the goal is to obtain 360-degree views of their customers, spanning all channels of distribution. This holistic view enables them to better serve customers with personalized experiences based on each individual's behavior and preferences. This view results in higher customer satisfaction, higher conversion, and deeper loyalty. On the operational side, the more retailers and CPG companies know about their customer needs, the better they're able to improve supply-chain planning and inventory management. They can use predictive analytics to forecast demand, and they can run what-if scenarios to optimize pricing.

Retailers, in particular, are able to slice and dice in-store and regional reporting to compare performance metrics and optimize inventory levels. They can easily analyze promotional data and share it with their CPG partners. And they can reduce costs related to product waste and inefficient staffing.

E-commerce companies and online divisions of multi-channel retailers can use technologies to track and analyze the individual checkout experience and understand the reasons for shopping cart abandonment. The technologies also enable real-time recommendations and promotions.

CPG companies can integrate shopper, retail, social media, and advertising data to more deeply understand consumer trends. In addition, sharing technologies enable them to share data easily with retail and advertising partners.

POWER SHIFTS TO THE CONSUMER

Retailers (and consumer-products brands) have to change the way they relate to customers—or suffer the consequences. Up until a few years ago, the most successful retailers and brands were in a dominant position, thanks to the power of television advertising and top retailers' ability to capture choice physical locations. They could tell consumers what to want.

Today, social networks and always-on personal technologies have shifted the power almost entirely to the consumer. That forces retailers and brands into an uncomfortable position in the customer conversation—as the listener. Consumers dictate now, and companies that don't listen to their customers and adapt to the change in the balance of power may be doomed to failure.

This is how Amazon has been conducting itself all along. Amazon's mission statement is as wide as the river it's named after: "We strive to offer our customers the lowest possible prices, the best available selection, and the utmost convenience." Amazon's goal is to be the most consumer-centric company in the world, and many retailers have been compelled to adopt a relentless focus on their customers, as well. They must know their customers better, listen to them, and respond quickly.

Some retailers in the United States have succeeded by focusing on a slice of the consumer population and serving it well. Examples are Dollar General, which caters to a lower-income customer, and Tractor Supply, which serves farmers, ranchers, and other people in rural areas. Others serve a wide variety of customer segments—such as Walmart, Target, and J. Sainsbury. The challenge for these retailers is to leverage data to understand the needs of each individual customer segment and to focus on the ones that drive their business.

Knowing customers better so you can serve them better is one of the areas where technology plays a critical role.

J. SAINSBURY'S JOURNEY

J. Sainsbury has put a high value on data ever since Mike Coupe became

CEO in 2014. His successor, Simon Roberts, CEO as of June 2020, is equally committed to exploiting the power of data and to keeping customers at the center of every decision J. Sainsbury makes. During Coupe's reign, J. Sainsbury began to rapidly consolidate the data from its subsidiaries: Sainsbury's supermarkets and convenience stores, Argos general merchandise, Tu clothing, Habitat home goods, and Sainsbury's Bank. The company put all the data in a Snowflake data platform in the cloud. The goal is to have everybody pool their data, breaking down brand and functional data siloes so they can enhance the customer experience.

The company gathers information about customers in a variety of ways. Its Nectar loyalty program, with 19 million members, cuts across all the store brands. It collects a vast amount of information about the shopping experience through its Lettuce Know program, which offers weekly prizes of Nectar points when customers fill out a survey that includes topics ranging from customer service to product availability. The company introduced a Lettuce Know smartphone app last year that enables it to collect feedback for particular locations instantly, as a customer leaves the store. Its e-commerce website, https://www.sainsburys.co.uk, sells products from all of the brands, and is another fountain of data.

J. Sainsbury uses data intensively across business functions. On the consumer-facing side, it supports decisions about pricing, merchandising, promotions, and individualized offers. But it also uses data to manage store operations and logistics—based in large part about what kind of person shops in a particular store. Some stores have more traditional checkout stations; others focus on self-checkout with mobile phones. Within a particular store, based on its footprint, they use data to figure out how to manage the stocking of shelves, with a goal of minimizing the time that a clerk is stocking rather than interacting with customers.

J. Sainsbury identified three types of internal users of its data—data scientists, professional analysts, and "citizen analysts," such as store managers, who don't have technical skills but still want to gain insights from data. Then the company designed a system that would accommodate all three.

While a big focus is on improving human decision making, one of Helen Hunter's goals is to increase the use of instrumentation and machine-to-machine messaging. When possible, she wants to make faster and better decisions by augmenting and reducing human decision making in business processes and for data to automatically trigger changes in operations. "I believe we're at a Gutenberg moment in the retail industry," she says. "I believe that a truly data-centric organization is one in which you have instrumented every one of your systems and processes and decisions so you can interrogate the data and optimize your operations."

Automation also helps the company stay attuned to its customers' attitudes. It uses artificial intelligence to read and interpret thousands of pages of comments it collects through its various listening mechanisms. The technologies identify issues customers are concerned about and sort them by their importance and urgency. When the data showed more customers described themselves as gluten-intolerant, the company added gluten-free baked-in-store items to its offerings.

All of this knowledge of shoppers' behavior, as individuals and in aggregate, also enables J. Sainsbury to become something of a trusted adviser to its customers. Because many customers have expressed interest in improving their diets, the company suggests healthier food choices and even offers recipes.

J. Sainsbury lives in a tough neighborhood, but Hunter is optimistic about the company's prospects. Says Hunter:" "I genuinely believe that the digital transformation backed up by the data transformation we're going through will be the thing that helps us win."

IMPROVING EFFICIENCIES WITH DATA

In retail, profit margins are often razor thin, so it's essential for retailers to operate ultra-efficiently. Technology can make the difference here, as well.

Take Office Depot, a leading provider of business services, products, and technology solutions to small, medium-size, and enterprise businesses. The company carried out a number of initiatives as it transformed itself into a fully integrated B2B distribution platform with more than 1,000 stores, an online presence, and dedicated sales professionals and technicians. Those initiatives include equipping store, warehouse, and delivery employees with mobile devices that put information at their fingertips. The company is also using Internet-of-Things technologies to optimize how it organizes products in its warehouses.

Undergirding Office Depot's business initiatives is a major shift in how it handles data. The company has moved all its data for analytics to the cloud, where it is managed via Snowflake's data platform.

The cloud switchover came in response to an unsustainable situation. Just a few years ago, Office Depot kept all its data in its own data center. Because of the large amount of data, its legacy analytics systems could get overwhelmed on particularly busy days. Analysts faced long wait times for answers to their questions.

By shifting to the cloud, Office Depot no longer had to purchase and manage its own data-center computers and storage devices. With Snowflake, it was able to consolidate three data management systems into one. The company pays for computation only when it uses it. "You get a massive Ferrari system when you need it, but it goes away when you don't need it," says Tim Nelson, the company's director for enterprise data and intelligence.

Office Depot keeps all its data in one place—everything from sales and inventories to costs and shipping information. As a result, store managers and financial analysts can instantly determine the profitability or loss coming from an individual order or transaction. In addition, because of the way Snowflake charges for computing services and storage, Tim can accurately forecast the costs of each of the company's analytics initiatives. With everything they do, they can move quicker. "We get ideas, we get alignment, and we go," he says.

THE JOYS OF DATA SHARING

So far, these examples of retailers capitalizing on data have focused on uses that take place within the four walls of a company. But there is another important dimension: sharing data between companies.

Data sharing is a major factor in relationships between retailers and consumer packaged goods companies. Most large retailers already interact with their supplier partners, but mainly through systems that use old technology, which can be expensive and slow.

Typically, they share point-of-sale data with partners by transferring via FTP sites. The partners have to download the data, convert it into forms that are digestible by their computing systems, and then do their analysis. There is a lag time of days or even weeks that prevents the retailer and its partners from responding quickly to changes in the market. Also, the sheer volume of data these days can become a logistical nightmare.

A cloud data platform can solve these problems. The retailer places all its data in the cloud and shares pieces of it with its supplier partners. Data capacity is unlimited, and there is no waiting for answers. Everybody has access to the system at the same time.

Sharing data also enables retailers and their suppliers to collaborate closely to improve the mix of products on the shelves or in online sales inventories. Retailers can't be expert in every product category, so often they rely on collaboration with strategic partners to ensure they are meeting customer needs. Enhanced data-sharing capabilities streamline this collaboration and allow decisions to be made much more quickly and efficiently.

Data sharing helps in another way, as well. Not every retailer has the capability for gathering large amounts of information about individual customers. It's difficult for them to get that 360-degree view. That's where a data exchange comes in.

Take the example of a retailer that does not have a loyalty program. When a customer comes through the checkout line and runs a credit or debit card through the point-of-sale register, the store gets very little information about the person. However, they can use a data exchange to connect with suppliers of information that can help fill out shoppers' profiles.

One data provider on the Snowflake exchange, Environics Analytics, provides demographic data derived from United States and Canadian census records. Its catalog includes wealth and household spending data, among other data types. By leveraging these privacy-compliant sources of information and combining them with data from points of sale, our retailer can build detailed customer personae. With these profiles, it can design marketing strategies for individual customers.

The massive transformation of the retail industry that began in the 1990s is still playing out. In addition, the coronavirus poses an existential threat to many retailers. This is truly a Darwinian moment.

To recover, retailers will have to make smart investments in analytics and other technologies to drive improvements in marketing, pricing, personalization, and delivery. After the crisis wanes, because of intense competition, they will still be under pressure to continually reinvent themselves. An essential element of reinvention is trying out new data management technologies that keep them in the game or, better yet, give them an edge.

12

FINANCIAL SERVICES

PICTURE a 25-year-old woman living in New York City and working as an associate attorney at a white-shoe law firm. The work hours are brutal—sometimes fifteen per day—so she has to keep her personal life simple. There's no time, for instance, to go to the bank. Instead, she prefers to use mobile and digital banking tools such as Eno, the intelligent assistant from Capital One.

Our lawyer uses Eno to pay bills and view her checking, savings, and credit card account balances. With Eno's virtual card number feature, the attorney is able to shop online without using her real credit card number. At checkout, Eno instantly creates virtual card numbers right from a browser so cardholders can keep their actual card numbers safe. If a suspicious charge comes in, Eno alerts her immediately via a text and she's even able to respond in natural language. And our lawyer, who happens to be a budding philanthropist, is overjoyed when Eno sends her an emailed summary of possible charitable donations that may be eligible for tax deductions at the beginning of tax season. All in a day's work.

Eno was built on top of the bank's cloud data platform and uses artificial intelligence to improve its performance. Data and analytics guided the design of Eno, and they support its everyday interactions with customers.

Eno is just one small piece of a massive, multi-year digital transformation that Capital One has undertaken.

"We're putting the customer at the center of everything we do," says Linda Apsley, former vice-president for data engineering at Capital One. She has since left the company. "We want to make their data available to them, and we want to give them the financial information that's useful for their lives."

The financial services industry is aggressively adopting new data analytics technologies based in the cloud. It's also rapidly migrating its data to the cloud. Capital One was one of the first big banks to declare its commitment to cloud computing and the first one to go "all in" on the public cloud. And now other banks are following suit. They are counting on the cloud not just for personalizing their interactions with customers but to help them navigate a rapidly changing—and unpredictable—business landscape.

FACING AN UNCERTAIN FUTURE

The industry took years to climb out of the black hole created by the global financial crisis of 2008, but early in 2020 it was stronger than ever by some measures. Until the coronavirus began its spread, Wall Street and other investment hubs were thriving. Now that the virus has taken hold around the world, there's a tremendous amount of uncertainty about the future direction of the market. Meanwhile, banks, especially in the United States, had been performing well—for the most part fending off or adapting to challenges from the emerging fintech industry. Now the virus is stressing them, as well.

Looking ahead to the next decade, uncertainty reigns. We won't know for months what the full impact of the virus will be. Among the longer-term macroeconomic challenges to the global financial services industry are political instability in a host of countries, climate change, and the backlash against globalization. If healthcare access increases in the United States, it could be a boon for insurance companies. But if Medicare for All takes hold, insurance companies will face massive disruptions.

While consumer-facing banks beat back the first wave of consumer fintechs, the establishment players now face competition from some of the giants of the tech industry, including Google, Apple, Facebook, and Amazon. Google signed a deal with Citigroup last year to develop a checking account that will be linked to Google Pay, its smartphone payment system. Apple launched its first iPhone-integrated credit card with Goldman Sachs. Watch this space.

CAPITALIZING ON THE DATA CLOUD

No matter what happens, the Data Cloud will likely be a critical asset for financial services companies—and their emerging competitors—in responding to the challenges and opportunities to come. "Financial-services companies are effectively data and analytics companies," says Matt Glickman, vice president for Snowflake Data Marketplace and customer product strategy. "That's their job: taking data, processing data, making decisions on data. They're making money for themselves and their clients based on data."

Snowflake has dozens of customers in financial services, running the gamut of industry segments. The technology trends in the industry are clear. After dragging their feet earlier, financial services companies are rushing to put the data in the cloud. That's driven in part by the efficiencies and responsiveness of cloud data technologies, but also by the ability to protect and manage data better and comply with new government privacy regulations on cloud data platforms like Snowflake's.

To respond to the challenges and uncertainties that financial services companies face in the coming years, the industry is investing heavily in data analytics technologies, particularly in artificial intelligence. Those that deal directly with consumers are improving their abilities to personalize interactions and products. And they are analyzing customer behavior to create new offerings. Practically across the board, financial companies are using data analytics to optimize the key competitive factors in their businesses, from loan interest rates and banking fees to the pricing of insurance products.

Here's how some of the financial services segments are using the Data Cloud:

RETAIL AND COMMERCIAL BANKING: Banks are using data analytics to identify branches and regions that are under- or overperforming. They're picking the best locations for branches and ATMs. They're also evaluating the performance of their products, from credit cards to certificates of deposit.

INVESTMENTS AND ASSET MANAGEMENT: Money managers are analyzing internal and external data to spot superior investment opportunities. They can better predict future trends and events by crunching massive amounts of historical data and doing "what if" analysis.

INSURANCE: They're able to improve their ability to spot fraud, to respond to new regulatory accounting requirements, and to more accurately price policies by micro-segmenting customers.

LENDING: Banks and specialty lenders previously relied on credit scores to evaluate applications for loans. Now they're able to consider a host of other factors, including information from social media posts. They're also better able to identify customers who are at risk of default so they can help them avoid it.

FINTECH: The primary interface between fintech companies and their customers is smartphone apps. Some fintech companies are building customer-facing apps on top of the Snowflake cloud data platform. Fintechs are using click-path data to improve the user interfaces and navigation features on their apps.

CAPITAL ONE'S BIG SHIFT

Capital One began exploring cloud computing in 2013. After George Brady joined as chief technology officer in 2014, the company had just opened its eighth data center and was beginning to move some applications and data to private cloud environments within its computing facilities. The following year, Capital One decided to go bold and migrate all of the company's computing to the public cloud. Senior executives saw the cloud as a powerful platform for innovation and the cornerstone of the company's digital transformation. "We think of ourselves as a customer-centric tech company that provides innovative financial services, not the other way around," says Brady.

Since then, Capital One has been shutting down data centers. The last three were to be shuttered this year. It now has thousands of business analysts and data scientists querying data stored in the cloud every day. Capital One is applying machine learning to almost every facet of its business, including call center operations, back-office process, fraud detection, cybersecurity, and credit monitoring.

For example, the bank is using machine learning to completely transform how it delivers curated, personalized experiences. Snowflake's cloud data platform enables the bank to put massive amounts of diverse datasets in one place where it can be worked on by machine-learning algorithms. The process improves fraud detection while reducing false positives that might lead to customers' cards being mistakenly locked.

Machine learning also plays a key role in the Eno app. Eno reads text and numbers. One of its newest features is its ability to review a customer's credit card transactions and draw inferences. For instance, it can spot charitable contributions the customer has made to nonprofits—which may be tax deductible. In advance of the tax return deadline, it alerts the customer of the charitable contributions she made during the calendar year so she can be sure to include them in her tax calculations.

HOW FINTECHS USE THE DATA CLOUD

The fintech phenomenon was born in 2009, when Australian John Reich started BankSimple (now just called Simple), the first of the so-called neobanks. Other digital banking startups followed. They were soon joined by startups that focused on investing and other financial services—all delivered by smartphone.

The phenomenon was seen as a wake-up call for an industry that was still in the early phases of recovery from the financial crisis. Some pundits predicted the demise of mainstream banking, but it didn't happen. One of the main challenges for the fintechs is that they are trying to establish themselves in a heavily regulated industry. It's difficult to operate like a bank if you don't have a banking license, so they typically forge alliances with established banks.

There have been a number of high-profile technology glitches as well. For instance, the Robinhood stock trading app went down three times in a single week in early March 2020, during a stock market meltdown over coronavirus fears. Robinhood's customers were not able to respond to the free fall in the markets.

One of the fintechs that shows staying power is Chime. It offers its members access to full-featured FDIC-insured spending and savings accounts, and to a Visa debit card on behalf of its banking partners, The Bancorp Bank and Stride Bank. With a mission to help its members achieve financial peace of mind, Chime's features include fee-free overdraft protection and an optional automatic savings program that rounds up spending account purchases and automatically deposits the change into the member's savings account. Chime has enabled more than 8 million accounts, making it the largest brand in its category. Most of Chime's revenue comes from interchange fees. Over time, Chime will expand into other areas within consumer financial services, including credit building.

Chime uses Snowflake for gathering and managing data from more than a dozen sources. That includes semi-structured data from Google and Facebook. By analyzing such complex data, Chime can identify ways to enhance the overall member experience.

Just as Chime offers new easy-to-use banking services for individuals, Square, another Snowflake customer, launched with the goal of making it easier for very small businesses to handle financial transactions and other financial matters. Founder Jack Dorsey wanted to empower people to start their own micro-businesses, but the company's products and services proved compelling for all kinds of customer-facing businesses, from stores and restaurants to beauty parlors and art galleries.

Square's first product was a point-of-sale device to process credit card transactions more conveniently and cheaply. The hardware pieces are a touchscreen and a scanner to enable payments and receipts. The company later expanded its offerings to include an array of services for small businesses, including loans, payroll management, customer relationship management, inventory management, and invoicing. Reporting and data analytics are built in.

Square's next move was to offer a portfolio of financial services for consumers. This includes debit cards, a rewards program, direct money transfers to individuals, and even the ability to buy and sell cryptocurrencies.

Snowflake's cloud data platform is an essential piece of Square's technology infrastructure. The company manages all of its operational data there and uses it to make decisions of all kinds. Square's leaders get daily updates on dashboards showing how all the products are performing, what level of customer engagement they're getting, and updates on fraud and risk. The engineering team monitors usage patterns in stores and on the apps to look for ways to improve the business owner and customer experiences. "It does everything in our data world. Everybody has come to rely on it," says Randy Wigginton, senior director for platform infrastructure engineering at Square.

WALL STREET: DATA CAPITAL OF THE WORLD

New York's financial services firms run on data—powering their trading, brokerage, investment advisory, asset management, wealth management, and investment banking businesses. We talked about the hedge fund Coatue at the beginning of Chapter 7. Other Wall Street firms have begun to adopt Snowflake's cloud data platform, often to support new business initiatives.

Wall Street firms of all stripes rely on data feeds from third-party providers. For trading, advisory services, and even investment banking, the organizations that have the most diverse, timeliest, and most accurate data have competitive advantages. Many of these organizations have hundreds of data feeds coming in, but almost all of them rely to a great extent on Bloomberg and its terminals for their core corporate and markets data. They receive Bloomberg data feeds, and they slice and dice the data, in part, with tools provided by Bloomberg.

Bloomberg does not have a true monopoly on the markets data business, but most financial services firms subscribe to its services. They feel they have to. At $20,000 to $24,000 per terminal per year, you can see how owner Michael Bloomberg's net worth is estimated to be north of $55 billion. Currently, there are about 325,000 Bloomberg terminal subscriptions worldwide.

Bloomberg is an aggregator of data. The company purchases it from organizations that generate it—including equities, bonds, and commodities markets around the world. Then it packages the data, marks it up, and delivers it to all sorts of financial professionals.

We talked briefly in Chapter 7 about the potential for the Snowflake data exchanges to disrupt traditional data flows by enabling data consumers to skip the middleman and purchase data directly from the sources. This is feasible because of the features of the Snowflake cloud data platform: easy sharing, no storage charges for consumers, and no computing charges for the data providers. Snowflake's platform makes it possible to disintermediate the middleman and unbundle data.

For data consumers, this is a big deal. "They had to pay this heavy tax to get their data, and now that tax can effectively go away," says Matt Glickman. Plus, with the data exchange model, they do not pay for data storage, and they only pay for computing when they need it.

For data generators, it's a way to control the distribution of their data and increase their revenue streams. "This breaks the monopoly," says Matt. "Now anyone can publish data directly out to the world at scale without an aggregator."

That's data unleashed—and it could turn out to be a very big deal for the financial services industry.

13

GOVERNMENT AND EDUCATION

N 2018, the State of California made one of the most aggressive save-the-planet moves yet by any government: It vowed that by 2045 all electricity supplied to end customers would come from renewable energy and zero-carbon sources. Accomplishing that goal will take the cooperation of energy suppliers, government agencies, scientists, businesses, and 40 million Californians.

The state now gets about 44 percent of its electricity from renewable sources, including 15 percent from hydroelectric, 10 percent from solar, and 9 percent from wind.

The California Energy Commission, the state's primary energy policy and planning agency, has been charged with gathering and managing the data that will support this effort. The Commission will gather a large volume of data from diverse sources, and it has chosen Snowflake's cloud data platform for managing the data.

California has adopted a cloud-first information technology strategy, and Governor Gavin Newsom has directed state agencies to be data driven in setting policies and making decisions.

The first step for this initiative is developing a comprehensive plan for accomplishing the zero-carbon goal. State government leaders will use the data they gather to evaluate technologies and forecasts to assess what must be done to maintain the reliability, safety, and affordability of the energy supply. They will size up potential costs and benefits to consumers. And they will develop several scenarios through which the goal can be achieved—presenting the costs and benefits of each scenario.

The California energy initiative signals that government agencies, which are often slower than businesses to adopt new technologies, are at last embracing the cloud. That means the flexibility and economies of cloud computing will be available to help solve some of the world's biggest problems, including climate change and global health and hunger issues. "We want to help change the world, and we're doing it with data," says Zach Oxman, a Snowflake government technology expert.

Government agencies face a conundrum. They routinely collect and store massive quantities of information, yet they typically do not possess the most up-to-date technologies for data management. They have gold nuggets in the ground, but they do not have the best tools to mine them.

There are numerous barriers to progress. The data government agencies collect is typically controlled by those agencies and too often kept in isolation, making it difficult for others to use it. Governments follow procurement processes designed to assure that they are getting the best value for the money, but that frequently means it takes them a long time to purchase and install new technologies. Also, because of aversion to risks, they are often reluctant to shift to new technologies that might be less expensive and more useful. Many of them still own and operate their own computers and data centers.

"We believe it's only a matter of time before the government gets comfortable with the cloud. We have to convince them and re-convince them. It's a process," says Rohit Dhanda, who heads federal government sales in the United States for Snowflake.

There are some signs that government leaders are changing their attitudes. As the California example shows, some believe it's important to be data driven and it's time to move to the cloud. Other states have adopted similar policies. For instance, Florida Governor Ron DeSantis reorganized the state's IT agency and put an increased focus on cybersecurity and cloud data technologies. Meanwhile, the federal government in 2015 launched a new IT strategy that encourages agencies to use the cloud—and grades them on their progress. That policy is slowly gaining traction.

Another positive factor: Around the country there is a movement within government to focus more on the outcomes of investments and practices. Voters are holding political leaders accountable for results. Agencies have been very good at gathering data. Now they recognize that they have to turn data into insights and insights into actions that help them run more efficiently and address critical issues such as the coronavirus, education quality, affordable housing, and the opioid crisis.

There is a bright side to the fact that government agencies have been slow to migrate their data to the cloud. Unlike a lot of Silicon Valley companies and large corporations, they did not jump on the Hadoop bandwagon. That approach to crunching data, which at one point seemed to show so much promise, turned out to be a major disappointment for many of the organizations that tried it. They set up their own specialized data centers for this purpose, which were very costly, and they discovered that the technologies were complex and difficult to master and manage. By being late, government agencies can leapfrog to the Data Cloud.

Snowflake's government IT experts have been exploring the potential for exploiting the Data Cloud with a number of federal and state government agencies in the United States. They have identified key reasons why a cloud data platform like Snowflake's could be particularly useful for government agencies. Here are some of them:

THERE ARE NO LIMITS: Cloud data platforms have essentially unlimited capacity for storing and analyzing data. Any number of analysts and leaders can access data concurrently. When a huge project comes along, like, say, the Census, the agency responsible for handling it can ramp up quickly to handle the data tsunami.

IT'S EASIER TO SHARE DATA: Once an organization's data is in one place, people in sister agencies can view and use the data—but without making copies. Today, many government agencies still share information by using FAX machines or by placing it on DVDs and popping them in the mail. Those days should be long gone.

THE CLOUD IS SIMPLE AND COST EFFECTIVE: No more buying and maintaining computer hardware and software. With Snowflake and others, the services are available on demand. You pay only for what you use. Privacy, security, and data governance are also easier managed within a cloud data platform.

THE CLOUD IS FASTER: In the federal government, the mantra is "time to mission." Agencies are under pressure to get things done quicker. They do not have the luxury of waiting around for two or three years for an IT integrator to build a new computing system before they start to get results. Today, it takes a year or more for many government annual reports to be published. The data can be out of date when it is released. The cloud can help address that issue.

Despite the advantages of cloud data analytics, government agencies and the technology providers that cater to them have to follow rigorous multistep processes before the keys to the cloud can be handed over. For instance, tech vendors attempting to sell cloud-based technologies to the federal government must undergo a seven-step process, involving third-party assessors, to become authorized under the FedRAMP program to compete for federal contracts. It can take months, if not years, to gain approval. Then there is a separate procurement process for each purchase by a federal agency. States have similar processes.

Don't expect a rapid uptake in the adoption of cloud computing in government agencies. However, when it happens, the shift to the Data Cloud has the potential to make governments much more efficient and much more responsive to the needs of the people they serve.

THE FEDERAL GOVERNMENT

You may be familiar with the controversial Department of Defense JEDI project. It's a contract worth up to $10 billion over ten years to provide cloud data analytics technologies to improve U.S. troops' access to intelligence in war zones. Amazon had been the frontrunner in the competition, but the government awarded it to rival Microsoft last October. Amazon filed suit. The project could be hung up for months or years. Still, it is a strong signal that the feds are committed to large-scale adoption of cloud computing.

Other federal agencies are exploring strategic use of cloud computing, including for national security, healthcare, and treasury programs. While some of the projects will use so-called private clouds—where their data is segregated because of concerns over secrecy—others are able to put data in the more economical public clouds.

Fraud, waste, and abuse are the plagues of government. Whether it's U.S. military procurement, Medicare and Medicaid reimbursements, or the Internal Revenue Service, large and complex government agencies and programs are ripe for abuse by crooks. In addition, across all departments, every year, there are tens of billions of dollars in spending for which government auditors can't account. They know the money was spent by somebody, somewhere, for something—but that's it.

Take Medicaid, the program for paying for healthcare for poor people. The dollars are hard to track and reconcile because it is a combined program of the federal government and all the states. The states report

Medicaid billings to the federal government on a regular basis. Then the feds have to analyze the data looking for patterns that might suggest fraud. The advantage of moving all this data to a cloud data platform is that as soon as the states enter their billing data into their computing systems, federal fraud investigators are able to view all the data together and can more easily spot anomalies—for example, fraudsters filing claims for the same patient in different states on the same day.

Data Cloud technologies can also help intelligence services and the military collaborate to deal with threats to American troops in the field. Intelligence services and branches of the military gather information for their own use. The intelligence agency that monitors phone calls stores its records in one data center. The folks running drones put their records in another. Combat units have their own data repositories. As a result, it's difficult for them to share intelligence. By pooling all their information immediately on a cloud data platform, they can triangulate and detect threats. Perhaps there is evidence from phones and drones that a bomb was recently planted along a certain road in Afghanistan that an infantry unit is about to walk down. Analysts connect the dots. Lives are saved.

"There are three problems that intelligence and military organizations have to overcome so they can collaborate more effectively: people, policies, and pipes," says Nick Speece, a Snowflake government expert who formerly served in the Air Force in Afghanistan and Iraq. "A cloud data platform gives them the data pipes so people can follow policies and communicate openly with one another."

STATE AGENCIES

States face a host of problems and needs, but they are not waiting around for the federal government to rescue them. Across the country, responsive state governments are grappling with issues ranging from healthcare and sea level rise to judicial reform.

Several states are taking on cash bail practices. The argument is that the cash bail system unfairly incarcerates people who have not been convicted of a crime. Reform advocates say the system punishes poor people for being poor. Bail payments allow someone accused of a crime to leave jail while they wait for their case to go to court. If individuals can't make bail, they stay in jail. They can't work and support their families. There is a negative impact on state finances, as well, since keeping people in jail is expensive.

The Data Cloud can be used to create pretrial risk assessment systems that enable judges and prosecutors to evaluate the likelihood of a person appearing for trial. Such a system could pool information about arrests and convictions from across a state and even, potentially, from across the country. The data would be made available in real time, and data analytics could be applied to score each individual based on their past criminal history and life situation. People with low risk scores could be released from court on their own recognizance.

State agencies also see a lot of potential in harvesting data from the Internet of Things. They are attaching networked sensors to devices and physical structures to monitor activities where it is unfeasible for humans to do the work. Think of the sensors as electronic eyes. This technology is already in wide use for automated highway toll tracking and billing systems. Increasingly, state public safety agencies see opportunities to spot and quickly react to safety hazards.

Data from sensors can be combined with real-time traffic data from vehicle navigation apps, and with police, weather, and public works data. Traditionally, all these datasets have been collected and stored in separate databases across a number of state agencies. Now, by using a cloud data platform, public safety officials can orchestrate their responses to problems on the roadways. If they detect hard braking on a section of highway, it might signal that there has been a collision—or one might happen soon. That way, police, fire, and EMTs can react quickly to save lives and minimize traffic delays. If a big winter storm is coming, data can tell public works officials where to deploy plowing equipment to get out ahead of it.

Only by combining the data can agencies create a true, timely picture of what's happening on the highways. This pooling of data requires a data management system that can combine a variety of data types from a variety of sources. Because so much data is being generated by the IoT sensors, the agencies need a very large database to store it in. None of this is really practical except in the cloud.

MUNICIPALITIES

Municipal governments are in the cloud data management game, as well. They are adopting cloud data analytics to help create "smart cities." For instance, the transit agency in a major city in England uses the Snowflake cloud data platform to improve operational efficiencies for its system of bus, tram, and train transportation. More than 5.6 million journeys are made via the transport network each day.

Last year, the agency launched a contactless system that eliminates paper tickets. Now, each journey produces a wealth of data about shifts in demand. The agency's biggest challenge was capturing that information and analyzing it to gain insights—until it moved the data to the cloud. The agency now runs micro-simulations of its transport networks to spot shifts in travel patterns. It is able to tally the number of people entering and exiting stations during events such as soccer (football) matches and music concerts. That way, additional trams can be available before and after the events.

EDUCATION

Snowflake education experts have been working with universities to use the cloud data platform to improve their services for students, staff, and alumni. Some universities hope to gather all the information they have collected about each student from the time they apply to the courses they take and the grades they get. They might also gather information from social media. This gives them a three-dimensional profile of each student, which could help them create more personalized and adaptive learning experiences.

For instance, the data might help the university spot people who are in need of special services, or it might enable the school to suggest courses or majors for students who are undecided. It could even help them pair roommates who might be compatible. Interestingly, the schools are using cold, hard data to help provide a more nurturing experience.

Many of these engagements are in the exploratory stages, but one involving the University of Notre Dame signals the potential for cloud data analytics to have outsize impacts on how these institutions operate and the quality of the experiences they deliver. Notre Dame doesn't just have perennially good football teams. It's a top-flight teaching and research institution. And it relies heavily on the generosity of its 135,000 alumni to fund those missions.

For years, the university alumni relations team had relied on a traditional database to assist with targeted outreach to alumni. Getting data into the database was cumbersome. In addition, the team was not able to easily identify likely donors for specific campaigns so it could reach out to them quickly. Queries routinely took thirty to ninety minutes to complete, so often the staff had to run reports after normal business hours. One analyst even had a T-shirt made up that read "My Query is Running." She later had a new one made that read "My Query is Still Running."

Notre Dame switched to the Snowflake cloud data platform. It wanted zero system maintenance and to be able to have as many as 300 analysts querying the data concurrently during peak fundraising campaign periods. Queries that formerly took thirty minutes suddenly were done in sixty seconds. "We can now move from data to information to a decision ten times faster," says Chris Frederick, the university's business intelligence manager.

No word on whether the analyst has retired her T-shirts.

14

HEALTHCARE AND LIFE SCIENCES

PICTURE THIS SCENARIO: A 70-year-old California man is vacationing with his wife in Montana
when he suddenly feels weakness on his side and
his vision gets blurry. He has suffered a stroke. The couple
is about a four-hour drive from Helena, the state capital.

Fortunately for him, his wife is able to drive him to a
clinic in a nearby town where the staff connects him via
computer with a stroke specialist in California. The physician prescribes a clot-busting drug, then the man is heli-
coptered to a hospital in Helena for advanced tests. The
tests confirm that he had a stroke but also show that blood
flow has been restored to his brain. Later, back home in
Bakersfield, California, he is referred to a neurologist for
continuing care.

The traveler is fortunate to be served by a healthcare system that operates a network of clinics and hospitals scattered across the Western states. The orchestrated response
to his medical emergency may have saved his life. It's an

example of the quality of care that can be delivered even under difficult circumstances by a well-managed healthcare organization that is dedicated to providing care wherever its patients may be.

A strategic element in this organization's approach to providing high-quality and efficient care is its focus on data and data analytics. Like other healthcare institutions, it is constantly being pushed to provide better care with less reimbursement from insurance companies, Medicare, and Medicaid. Unlike many other healthcare systems, this one is transforming itself through smarter use of data. This scenario and this healthcare system are real, but we withheld the name and changed some of the details at the organization's request.

HEALTHCARE UNDER PRESSURE

You can think of this scenario as a microcosm of the challenges facing the healthcare system in the United States. In some ways, the system here is the envy of the world. People with good health insurance can typically choose their personal physicians and specialists, and they benefit from the most sophisticated diagnostic tools and best-targeted pharmaceuticals.

Yet in other ways, the system is failing. Many people are not covered by insurance. Others have poor access to high-quality medical care. Meanwhile, the costs for individuals, insurance companies, employers, and society are astronomical—much greater than the costs in other developed nations. National health expenditures in the United States grew 4.6 percent, to $3.6 trillion, in 2018, or $11,172 per person, accounting for nearly 18 percent of gross domestic product. Analysts at the U.S. Centers for Medicare & Medicaid Services expect those expenditures to hit $6 trillion by 2027. A December 2019 poll conducted by Gallup found that 25 percent of Americans say they or a family member have delayed medical treatment for a serious illness because of the costs of care.

At the same time, healthcare providers are under pressure to transition from fee-for-service financial models to outcomes-based approaches.

Everybody involved agrees that costs are unsustainable and that incentives need to change, but there is plenty of disagreement about what should be done about it.

There is widespread agreement, though, about one thing: Better use of data could help enable participants in the healthcare system to operate more efficiently and deliver better care. That includes all types of organizations—physician groups, hospitals, medical schools, health insurance providers, government health services, and pharmaceutical companies.

The coronavirus pandemic exposed the shortcomings of our healthcare systems and our public health strategies and resources, both in the United States and worldwide. Hopefully, government and healthcare leaders will learn lessons from this crisis and will make changes that improve their responses and the resiliency of society when new virus threats emerge. Data will surely play an important role in the decisions they make and the plans they lay.

As a result of the virus, the kind of telemedicine services described in our Montana scenario are being launched or expanded by healthcare organizations across the world. Cloud computing and the Data Cloud support these services.

Before the pandemic, healthcare data was projected to grow 36 percent annually over the next five years—faster than in any other major industry. That's largely because of the growth of data related to genomics, patient health and fitness monitoring, digital imaging, and the conversion of physicians' notes to digital formats. Many organizations are only now switching over totally to electronic medical records. This flood of data is a blessing and a curse. All the participants in a nation's healthcare system need to exploit data more effectively, and to do so they need to be able to manage data better and share data with each other more fluidly.

The Data Cloud provides easy access to large and diverse datasets. Cloud data platforms make it easier to integrate disparate types of data—

such as melding genomic data with electronic medical records. The economics of cloud storage make it possible to affordably store the genomic records for a large number of patients, and to capture vast amounts of information related to the social determinants of health. In addition, cloud data platforms provide security and data governance features that enable organizations to confidently share personal information across departments or with partners.

Todd Crosslin, the healthcare industry leader at Snowflake, says there is an opportunity to use data to help transform the way care is delivered in this country. It will enable a shift from a transactional view to one that focuses more on patients and their health journeys. "We want to focus more on the quality, the outcome," he says.

A CLOUD DATA PLATFORM FOR HEALTHCARE

Snowflake's executives and healthcare experts have been engaging with leaders in healthcare fields to identify the most powerful use cases for a cloud data platform. Here are a few of the most compelling scenarios:

360-DEGREE PATIENT VIEW: Just like advertisers and retailers are using data to craft 360-degree views of individual consumers, healthcare organizations have begun doing the same—charting the patient's journey. Physician groups and hospitals can combine EMRs, test results, physician notes, and genomic data to better diagnose diseases and choose treatments. If they learn that a patient needs to be reminded to take medication daily, they can alert them using texts or automated phone calls.

Dashboards and data visualizations created for patients and their families can help them understand diseases and treatments better. Risks can be presented in graphical forms, making it easier for people to decide among treatment options.

PRECISION MEDICINE: Thanks to genome sequencing, doctors can examine patients' genetic makeup for mutations that increase the risk of diseases. This makes it possible to treat individuals in very personalized ways. Physicians can choose the therapies that a person is most likely to respond to or even advise them to make lifestyle changes to avoid trouble later in life.

On the flip side, pharmaceutical companies can study the responses of people with various genetic dispositions to their drugs—helping them to design therapies to address cohorts of patients with similar clusters of gene mutations.

BRINGING NEW THERAPIES TO MARKET: It typically takes a decade and costs more than $1.5 billion to bring a new drug therapy to market. Cloud data platforms can help accelerate development, testing, and approvals in a number of ways.

Researchers can use machine-learning models to run simulations of how particular compounds could treat disease—or cause harmful side effects. In this way, they can test millions of combinations on the computer before they shift to animal testing.

Clinical trial managers can use data to help locate and enroll participants in their studies and to manage relationships with the patients while the trials are going on.

During trials, pharma companies can analyze large amounts of genomic data for each patient involved to figure out why the therapy is more effective for one patient than another. That way, physicians will know which patients are likely to benefit most from the drugs.

HOW HEALTHCARE PROVIDERS CAN USE DATA

Let's elaborate on the scenario we explored at the beginning of this chapter. Imagine that the healthcare system uses the Snowflake cloud data platform for managing a variety of data types, including physician notes and genomics information.

In the remote care arena, the organization gathers vital signs data from patients who live a great distance from clinics—helping them learn to use monitoring devices and then tracking their health status from afar. If a monitor sends a signal to the clinic that the blood glucose level has suddenly plunged for a patient with Type 2 diabetes, the clinic can automatically send an alert to the patient urging her to eat a snack.

The organization uses machine learning to evaluate how engaged each patient is with their care. By identifying patients who are likely to miss appointments or stop taking their medications, it is better able to predict which patients will need more attention from the office staff or clinicians. That way, the staff can reach out to potentially noncompliant patients to help them stay healthy.

Thanks to having a wide variety of data at their fingertips, clinicians can practice precision medicine. When meeting with patients, physicians ask questions of the computer system in everyday language and get instant answers that help them choose treatment options that are most likely to work for that particular patient.

Data helps the organization improve its efficiency. By loading and analyzing several years of patient care, cost, and reimbursement data, it can predict on a patient-by-patient level whether it will be reimbursed for a particular test or procedure. Armed with that information, a clinician can discuss options with the patient. If the patient knows that she will have to pay for a particular test out of pocket, she can discuss with the physician whether it's really clinically necessary. The hope is that this might cut down on unnecessary tests—without shortchanging patients who really need them.

Technology also helps prevent clinician burnout. The organization uses natural language processing and machine learning to relieve pressure on clinicians to manually enter information into EMRs. That way, doctors can focus on patients rather than keyboards.

A CLOUD DATA PLATFORM FOR
PHARMACEUTICALS

The pharmaceutical industry faces a host of challenges. It's getting more expensive to develop new drugs, competition from generics is increasing, and revenue growth has slowed for many companies. Meanwhile, the industry is under intense pressure to reduce the costs of drugs.

It's clear that the pharma industry has to find ways to reduce the cost and time required to discover new therapies and bring them to market.

Fortunately, the life sciences domain is awakening to the power of the Data Cloud. The rapid decrease in the cost of whole genome sequencing makes it possible to map the genes of hundreds of thousands and eventually millions of individuals. At the same time, researchers can tap into huge repositories of digitized phenotype information—the records of how genes express themselves in humans and how environmental factors affect health. We're talking petabyte-scale datasets.

A new business model is emerging for harnessing this data to improve the process of drug discovery. Companies that specialize in outsourcing drug discovery for pharmaceutical companies are investing in cloud data platforms and offering not just research services but also data analytics to their clients.

They are assembling vast data collections—including genomics, healthcare outcomes data, and biological knowledge. Since this approach requires a large amount of information drawn from a wide variety of sources, it is a natural fit for the Data Cloud. In fact, because of the size of the datasets and the scale of computing required, this kind of work is not sustainable using traditional approaches.

Traditionally, pharmaceutical companies and university researchers conduct their own research in-house, using data available to them, open-source software tools, and their own clusters of high-performance computers.

The third-party research specialists achieve economies of scale by assembling gigantic datasets, software tools, and cloud computing resources to be shared by large numbers of researchers from medical schools, large pharmaceutical companies, and biotechnology companies.

This approach could accelerate the process of identifying promising compounds for use in drug therapies. It also helps with identifying potentially crippling side effects from drugs and for discovering biomarkers that can help with disease prevention. Because of the efficiency gains, there is also a potential for reducing the price of drugs, or increasing the profits of drug companies, or both.

Healthcare experts at Snowflake believe that some of these research initiatives will reside on the company's private exchange platform. There, groups of complementary organizations can share data and tools even more conveniently. It's an environment optimized for collaboration, which is an essential ingredient in the drug discovery process.

There is also a role for cloud data analytics in helping pharmaceutical companies market their drugs. For instance, Symphony Health, a life sciences informatics company, recently launched a national market measurement tool, Metys, that integrates prescriber, payer, and patient datasets. Many drugs are used to treat a number of conditions or diseases. Using Symphony Health's tool, pharma companies can discover why each patient is using a particular product. If they learn that a drug is seldomly being prescribed for a disease that it is very effective at treating, they can launch marketing campaigns aimed at increasing its use for that purpose.

The healthcare industry is in the early stages of a data revolution, one that will transform the diagnosis and treatment of patients, the discovery of drugs, and the marketing of drugs to people who will benefit from them. Because of their efficiencies and data-sharing capabilities, cloud data platforms seem likely to play a critical role in enabling—and accelerating—this shift. Data will have sizable impacts on many industries. But because of the importance of healthcare to all of us, none will be as important as the impact on health.

15

THE DEMOCRATIZATION
OF DATA

HEATHER NIVENS calls herself a "data whisperer." She grew up on a farm north of Oklahoma City and got a PhD in agricultural economics at Kansas State, but, rather than making agriculture her career, she decided to wrangle large and complex datasets.

Over the past 20 years, she has worked at several companies, including FedEx, Boeing, and a law firm. Her career has followed the trajectory of the field of data analytics, arcing from Excel spreadsheets in earlier times to machine-learning algorithms today. "I like to find the answers to the off-the-wall questions that don't seem to have an easy answer. That's my sweet spot," she says.

Heather is the embodiment of one of the most significant trends in the business world today: the democratization of data. In the old days, only the largest or richest organizations had the resources to take advantage of the Big Data revolution and the power of data analytics. Now, thanks to the cloud and a host of new data analytics technologies, anybody with skills and training can be a data whisperer.

As a result, individuals can have a bigger impact on their organizations, and they can accelerate their careers. The same goes for people who are self-employed. In the case of Snowflake's technology, all you need is a credit card and a Snowflake account to get started. "You can be a one-man band and use Snowflake," says CEO Frank Slootman. "You don't even have to be a programmer per se with the onslaught of modern analytics and machine learning tools. You need some basic data skills, and you're off to the races."

Today, Snowflake has thousands of customers who purchase services on demand with credit cards. You can run a query in a few seconds and pay the price of a pizza.

At the same time, with the help of data analytics, small companies can become bigger companies faster. In Snowflake's early days, it marketed its products primarily to technology startups. Many had only a few dozen employees. Now, a number of those companies have hundreds of employees. Gaining access to this powerful technology in the cloud enables them to scale up rapidly without having to invest in expensive server computers. It also levels the playing field for them when they compete with larger companies.

In addition to all those on-demand customers, Snowflake had a lot of small and midsize customers that sign contracts and pre-pay for Snowflake credits, mostly to get a better discount.

About half of them are technology companies that build their products on top of Snowflake. In recent quarters, about 70 percent of the new technology-focused customers use Snowflake as a foundation for their own products—which shows that it's taking off as a development platform.

Another advantage for customers that are also technology partners is that once they are running on Snowflake, they can more effectively market their technologies to other companies that are also running their data on Snowflake. The service operates as a virtual marketplace.

Like other tech companies, Snowflake encourages the individuals who use its technologies to feel like they are part of a community. Originally, the company targeted business leaders for its community-building programs, but now it reaches out to all sorts of people, from developers and database administrators to software architects and data scientists. About 20,000 people are registered as members of the Snowflake community programs.

The company rewards individuals who voluntarily contribute to knowledge-sharing forums and community blogs. People who organize and run Snowflake meetups get special treatment. The company launched a "Data Heroes" program to reward frequent contributors with early invitations to Snowflake events and swag. The perennial favorite gift is a black Patagonia ski jacket with the little white Snowflake logo on it.

Here are profiles of some Snowflake users that give you a sense of the power of the democratization of data.

KAI WOLFFRAM

Kai, 35, runs a data analytics team for the hotel division of TUI, the world's largest travel company. In addition to booking and managing travel for consumers online and in stores, TUI owns more than 300 hotels and owns and operates its own cruise ships and passenger jets. Kai works in the company's headquarters in Hanover, Germany, where he manages a team of a dozen data analysts. Only one of his people has a PhD. "You don't need so much math and statistics knowledge now because the tools do so much for you," he says.

TUI has a strong cloud focus these days, but it wasn't always so. In fact, Kai was one of the people on the grassroots level who got things moving. Starting years ago, he led a team that managed the migration of the company's tour operations data from a traditional on-premises data warehouse to the cloud. After he moved over to run data analytics for the hotel business, he built a cloud data warehouse from scratch.

The hotel business analysts see fresh data every day from the hotels. Based on their knowledge of the guests and the amenities available at each location, they recommend offers for everything from room upgrades to day tours.

Kai is an active member of the Snowflake community. He has made marketing videos and runs webinars. Gratis. He just likes doing it. "I'm an ambassador for Snowflake's story and technology. I'm spreading the word," he says.

RANDY PITCHER

The boutique IT consulting firm that Randy works for, Hashmap, provides "data consulting for rebels," he says—meaning the company's clients are aggressively moving to the cloud to become more data driven. Hashmap, which is based in Atlanta, has shifted its focus from maintaining expensive and complex on-premises data warehouses to creating data pipelines and data management solutions in the cloud. "We're much more focused on solving business problems, since the maintenance is taken care of," says Randy, 27, who works in the firm's Oklahoma City office.

For Randy, one of the main attractions of Snowflake is that he and his analysts can use the popular and easy-to-use Structure Query Language (SQL) to execute sophisticated maneuvers that would have required complex actions using the Python or Scala programming languages. "There's a lot of cool technology out there that doesn't necessarily align with being useful," he says. "But this is both cool and incredibly useful. I feel like I'm riding the cloud wave. I'm on the right side of history."

Randy is such a Snowflake fan that he has taken it upon himself to organize monthly Snowflake meetups in Oklahoma City. When he started this a year ago, he would typically attract only a handful of attendees. Now he routinely gets twenty-five to thirty people, including, occasionally, the data whisperer, Heather Nivens.

ASHWIN NAYAK

Ashwin moved to the United States from India about 20 years ago. He had studied computer science at the University of Bangalore. Then he taught software programming in Bangalore before he went to work for a tech company. He saw firsthand the beginnings of the amazing rise of the Indian tech industry.

Now, Ashwin, 44, is vice president for engineering at Quaero, a data analytics company based in North Carolina. Quaero provides consumer marketing solutions, including personalization, across paid and owned media. Earlier, the software ran on specialized computing appliances. About a year and a half ago, Quaero learned that the computer company that made the appliances planned on getting out of the business. Quaero scrambled to find an alternative. It ended up making a major move, upgrading the platform with Snowflake.

Ashwin says the shift has given Quaero a clear path forward. The company has about 100 employees, but its move to the cloud and Snowflake enables it to compete with much larger companies. Plus, since Snowflake runs on all three major public clouds—Amazon, Microsoft, and Google—Quaero seems to be poised to grow as its customers accelerate their migration of data to the cloud. At the same time, it's able to keep its engineering costs low by relying on Snowflake to handle most of the complexity of running the software on three separate clouds.

Quaero's engineering team is based primarily in India, so Ashwin travels there a couple times a year. He expects cloud data analytics to provide yet another boost to India's tech industry. The largest Indian the cloud system, Nat says, the company can now give an account to any employee who wants one. "What we get out of data increased dramatically," he says.

CARLOS SOUSA

When Carlos, who grew up in a tiny village in the north of Portugal, was 10 he walked past the room in his school where the computer club met. It was his first sight of a personal computer, and he was smitten. Says Carlos: "I saw the kids using computers, and I understood that I could build stuff. I didn't need tools or materials. All I needed was my brain and a computer. It was a profound epiphany."

Now, at 35, he is head of product architecture for OutSystems, a technology company that was founded in Portugal but now has its headquarters in Boston. Carlos lives and works in Lisbon. The company sells a low-code software development platform.

The low-code approach enables the delivery of software applications faster and with minimal hand coding. Visualization techniques make it a great fit for professional developers who are focused on increasing productivity, as well as for people who lack computer science training. The company's products enable the democratization of application development. Now, practically anybody can do it.

Within OutSystems itself, any of the company's 1,200 employees can ask for permission to use the company's tools to develop Web and mobile applications to help them and their colleagues do their jobs better. There are active application makers in the sales, marketing, and HR departments.

OutSystems' engineers and their "citizen developer" colleagues are supplied not just with software tools but also with the data that will be used within the applications they are developing. The data comes from the cloud system, Nat says, the company can now give an account to any employee who wants one. "What we get out of data increased dramatically," he says.

CARLOS SOUSA

Carlos, who grew up in a tiny village in the north of Portugal, was 10 he walked past the room in his school where the computer club met. It was his first sight of a personal computer, and he was smitten. Says Carlos: "I saw the kids using computers, and I understood that I could build stuff. I didn't need tools or materials. All I needed was my brain and a computer. It was a profound epiphany."

Now, at 35, he is head of product architecture for OutSystems, a technology company that was founded in Portugal but now has its headquarters in Boston. Carlos lives and works in Lisbon. The company sells a low-code software development platform.

The low-code approach enables the delivery of software applications faster and with minimal hand coding. Visualization techniques make it a great fit for professional developers who are focused on increasing productivity, as well as for people who lack computer science training. The company's products enable the democratization of application development. Now, practically anybody can do it.

Within OutSystems itself, any of the company's 1,200 employees can ask for permission to use the company's tools to develop Web and mobile applications to help them and their colleagues do their jobs better. There are active application makers in the sales, marketing, and HR departments.

OutSystems' engineers and their "citizen developer" colleagues are supplied not just with software tools but also with the data that will be used within the applications they are developing. The data comes from

Snowflake's cloud data platform. Each user can select from a catalog of data that their role in the company enables them to access. It's simple. They drag and drop datasets into their applications.

Carlos sees this merging of developer tools and data as another huge step forward in the history of computing. It's epiphany worthy. "This is a good example of where the democratization of application development meets the democratization of data," he says. "This expands the number of people who can speak the data language and leverage it to create business value."

16

DATA FOR GOOD

FOR KENYA'S 3.5 million smallholder farmers, scraping out a living on a few acres of land is arduous and risky. Many of these tiny farms produce crops for a family and perhaps a few neighbors. During droughts and blights, people go hungry and sometimes are forced to eat the insects that feed on their crops.

Efforts to support farmers in their transition to more commercial forms of agriculture face a host of challenges as a result of farmers' small scale, difficulty in accessing markets, and lack of formal financial history leading to a paucity of credit with which to pay for seeds, pesticides, and fertilizer. Farmers have to buy the inputs before the rains begin, which dictates planting time. They don't get paid until after they have harvested and sold their crop, about 10 months later.

Victor Njue Njeru knows all too well the challenges of making a living on a small plot of land. He and his wife farm three acres in Embu County, about eighty miles northeast of Kenya's capital city, Nairobi. Victor, who is 50

VICTOR NJUE NJERU ON HIS FARM. SOURCE: APOLLO AGRICULTURE

years old, has been farming for twenty years. In the past, he lacked quality seeds and fertilizer, and he typically produced only about ten bags of corn, his main crop, per year.

Now, thanks to a series of loans from Kiva, a global microfinance organization, and Apollo Agriculture, a financing and products platform for small-scale farmers, Victor has nearly doubled his output. He is also investing in irrigation, and he has leased neighboring land to expand his operations.

"It has been a struggle," says Victor. "In the past, I had low yields. When I could, I borrowed money from a friend or sold a goat or a cow to pay for seeds and fertilizer. But it was never enough to really make a difference." Victor spoke in Kiswahili, and his comments were translated by Javan Felix, who is on the staff of Apollo Agriculture.

The money and assistance have been life-changing for Victor and his family. For one thing, he is able to pay tuition and other educational expenses for two of his children. One of them is in high school and the other is studying at a university. Victor says he is grateful to Kiva and Apollo Agriculture.

It happens that both organizations use data intensively to improve their operational efficiencies, expand their reach, and help regular people lift themselves up by their bootstraps. In other words, they use data for good.

THE DATA REVOLUTION BREAKS OUT

The data revolution is breaking out all over the place. It is changing the landscape for corporations, governments, universities, and healthcare systems. It empowers individuals, as we saw in the previous chapter. But it also helps people all around the world who have been disadvantaged by the legacies of colonialism, racism, warfare, and poverty.

Apollo Agriculture was founded in 2016 by Benjamin Njenga, Eli Pollak, and Earl St. Sauver. Eli and Earl had worked together previously at Climate Corporation, which advised large-scale farmers in the United States. After the company was sold, they decided to launch a company that would focus on helping small-scale farmers in developing countries maximize their profits—starting with Kenya.

"We wanted to partner with some of the world's most vulnerable people and help them double, triple, or quadruple their yields," says Eli, Apollo Agriculture's CEO. "Our mission is helping farmers make more money, and the way we do that is we help them access the products, services, insurance, and capital they need to make a transition from subsistence farming to commercial farming."

Climate Corporation was a heavy user of data analytics, and so is Apollo Agriculture. Because it is expensive and time consuming to serve thousands of farmers who are scattered across the countryside, Apollo Agriculture must run as efficiently as possible. It uses technology and data to optimize its operations—driving down the cost of customer acquisition and servicing. It gathers the data it needs to make credit decisions, to provide good advice, and to deliver physical products efficiently and scalably.

Assessing credit risks is especially challenging in a place where farmers don't typically keep detailed financial records or have relationships with banks. Traditional lending models in Kenya rely on group lending and large networks of on-the-ground field agents, which makes it difficult for Kenya's Credit Reference Bureau(s) to monitor individual credit. So, to build a credit profile, Apollo Agriculture collects information from interviews with farmers and people they do business with, and it uses satellite images to evaluate the potential for productivity gains on the farmer's land. Then it leverages artificial intelligence technologies, including machine-learning models developed in-house by a team of data scientists, to assess the farmer's creditworthiness.

Apollo Agriculture sells farmers a bundle of products, advice, training, and insurance. Each bundle is customized and priced for an individual farmer. The company arranges pay-back terms based on each farmer's ability to pay and estimated harvest time. Apollo raises working capital from a variety of sources to finance its lending portfolio. One of the significant sources is Kiva, which doesn't charge interest to farmers or fees to Apollo Agriculture. The two organizations share customers and data.

CROWDFUNDING FOR GOOD

While Apollo Agriculture is a startup, Kiva has been around since 2005. The organization was launched in San Francisco by a couple, Matt Flannery and Jessica Jackley, who were inspired by a 2003 lecture given at

Stanford Business School by Muhammad Yunus, founder of the microfinance pioneer Grameen Bank. While Grameen Bank, based in Bangladesh, is heavily dependent on field agents to make and service loans, Kiva relied from the start on technology and data to manage what soon became a global operation and a network of field partners who manage the loans.

Kiva raises money on its website from people who are willing to fund entrepreneurs without earning interest. Each entrepreneur is featured in a profile that describes her life, her business, and what she plans on doing with the money. The nonprofit organization is supported primarily by grants and donations. So far, Kiva has crowd-funded more than 1.8 million loans totaling $1.4 billion. It has a repayment rate of 97 percent.

A few years ago, though, Kiva's growth in lenders and borrowers leveled off. The organization had helped millions of borrowers, but, still, there were an estimated 1.7 billion adults in the world who did not have access to traditional banks and loans. To rekindle growth and increase the organization's impact, the board of directors in 2017 brought in a new CEO, Neville Crawley, who had a strong data analytics background. One of his first major hires was Ken Leung as executive vice president for engineering.

Ken had thirty years of technology leadership experience in companies large and small. Ken's wife had been lending through Kiva for a decade, and she loved the organization. When she learned that Kiva had reached out to him, she said: "Go work for them."

Kiva had begun using Snowflake's cloud data platform the year before Ken arrived. Previous to switching to Snowflake, Kiva's tech team had been using a data warehouse that required it to purchase and maintain computers—and to spend a lot of time tuning the database and programming queries. Its twenty-person software engineering team was stretched. By moving to the cloud and Snowflake, the organization didn't have to invest big bucks in hardware and its engineers didn't have to spend a lot of time keeping the data warehouse running properly. "Our strategy is to leverage the cloud so we can devote our resources to our core mission," says Van Mittal-Henkle, a senior software engineer who has been at Kiva since 2011.

The switch also made it possible for the tech team to experiment freely with new approaches to managing and analyzing data. Because Kiva didn't have to buy computers to increase its data processing capacity, its analysts could tap into computing resources in the cloud, use them intensively for a few minutes, and then switch off.

After Ken arrived, he took a fresh look at how Kiva was using technology overall—not just in data management. He accelerated the shift to cloud computing and focused on using cloud-native software, like Snowflake's.

Starting in 2019, Snowflake began offering discounts to nonprofit organizations, including Kiva. The idea came from Bob Muglia, Snowflake's previous CEO. "Bob believed we had a responsibility to help others. By offering our product at a discount, more nonprofits can use it, and it can help them fulfill their missions through better use of data," says David Hudanish, vice president and deputy general counsel at Snowflake, who helped design the discount program.

At Kiva, Ken didn't just add cloud technologies. He upgraded the staff's sophistication—adding data scientists to use machine learning to harvest better insights and do it faster.

"Kiva is in the business of moving money around the world. We are a marketplace that takes capital from one area and distributes it to another area. Our mission is to do good with that movement," Ken says. "We are using technology and data to increase our capacity to move money around and to increase our speed of moving money around."

In recent months, Kiva has been adding more real-time data to the Snowflake data warehouse. That includes detailed information about the behavior of visitors to the Kiva.org website. A particular interest is the tipping feature. One of the ways Kiva raises money to cover its administrative and operational costs is by asking lenders to add a tip to the loan with the understanding it will go to Kiva rather than to the borrower. The bigger the tips, the more Kiva can accomplish. Data scientists and user interface engineers experiment selectively with a small number of lenders to see if they can induce them to give bigger tips. They gather and analyze click data and see which experiments yield the best results.

PERSONALIZING THE LENDER'S EXPERIENCE

Kiva also uses cloud data to personalize a lender's experience on the Kiva.org website. Based on the characteristics of past loans, it offers each lender a different portfolio of potential new loans when she or he enters the website. If somebody has shown an interest in women entrepreneurs in Latin America, they'll see a different set of profiles than somebody who favors male farmers in Africa. Since many lenders tended to let money that had been paid back sit idle in their Kiva accounts, the organization is now automatically re-loaning the money to entrepreneurs who fit their lending preferences.

In addition, Kiva uses cloud data to analyze which field partners perform better. Based on that analysis, the organization distributes more or less money to particular partners.

One of Kiva's major new initiatives is the so-called Kiva Protocol, a digital identification system for small businesses in developing nations. This emerged as a way to deal with the fact that most small farmers and small business owners in those countries don't have relationships with banks. That makes it difficult for them to get loans, since it's hard for them to prove they are who they say they are, banks don't know them, and they don't have a documented track record of paying back loans.

Kiva announced Kiva Protocol in 2018 in partnership with the government of Sierra Leone and with the help of United Nations agencies. At the time, Sierra Leone had only one credit bureau serving 2,000 people.

An estimated 80 percent of the adult citizens are unbanked. The protocol is essentially a nationwide digital identification system. When the system is fully up and running, it will enable banks and informal lenders such as shopkeepers and suppliers to help contribute to a person's credit history.

Here's how it works: When a lender in Sierra Leone makes a loan, the system sends a signed digital document to the borrower's cell phone or to an agency the entrepreneur is working with. The borrower accepts the document and posts it to a credit ledger in their private digital wallet. When the borrower makes a payment, it is posted to the wallet. Only the lender and the borrower can see the records. If the borrower later wants to apply for a loan from a large bank, she grants the bank one-time access to her credit history. The system is very inexpensive to run, so it doesn't require borrowers to pay processing fees.

One of the criticisms of microfinance is that in some situations lenders charge borrowers interest rates that would be considered usurious if they were operating in the United States or Western Europe—sometimes more than 50 percent. That's because of the high costs of making and servicing their loans and high default rates. But systems like Kiva Protocol take costs and risks out of the equation, enabling lenders to lower their rates.

"Kiva Protocol is working to enable people to move up from a community lending circle to microfinance to a bank," says Matthew Davie, Kiva's chief strategy officer. "They will be building a data profile that they can use to further their way up the financial ladder so they have access to more equitable and more appropriate products and services. They won't be systematically excluded."

Kiva Protocol is just now getting off the ground in Sierra Leone, but, once it is running smoothly, Kiva plans on expanding to other countries in Africa and elsewhere through partnerships with national governments. Eli Pollak of Apollo Agriculture says: "Anything that moves the market in the direction of knowing your customer and helping people to build credit histories is good for customers, and what's good for customers tends to be good for us."

The Kiva Protocol makes use of some very sophisticated and cutting-edge technology. It uses a blockchain distributed ledger system to store and provide views into credit histories. That system assures that there is a single version of each record and the information can't be changed unless both parties agree to it.

Kiva has other innovative programs in development or in the planning stages. In each case, data analytics is expected to play a significant role in shaping new programs and measuring their effectiveness.

FUELING STRATEGIC INITIATIVES WITH DATA

When Matthew arrived in 2018, he was given the task of reviewing Kiva's strategic initiatives over the next five to ten years. He has focused on two vectors. First, he looked for opportunities to increase the organization's impact by expanding the use of secure, user-centric digital technologies. Kiva Protocol is an example. At the same time, he looks for ways to increase the amount of more formal capital that is available to those in need. That is where another new program developed by the team, Kiva Capital, comes in.

Kiva's traditional model of raising money from individual lenders and distributing it to specific borrowers is a proven means for giving people a toehold in the formal economy. But what happens after a borrower gets a series of small loans and repays them, demonstrating her creditworthiness? She is ready to scale up her business, but she needs larger loans. Through the Kiva Capital program, Kiva reaches out to global financial institutions and appeals to them to invest some of their so-called social impact funds, money they have set aside to help improve lives and communities. Kiva uses those funds, rather than small amounts raised from individual lenders, to lend to more mature businesses.

The organization plans on launching a series of institutional funds under the Kiva Capital program. It closed its first such fund, for refugees, in the spring of 2020. Kiva hopes to eventually follow up with funds for women, agriculture, and fast-growing small businesses.

With the arrival of the coronavirus pandemic and the disruptions to society around the world, Kiva's services were more important than ever. The organization hit pause on the repayment of loans in some places that were ravaged by the pandemic. On April 30, 2020, it introduced the Global COVID-19 Response fund, urging lenders to support COVID-19-related loans as they became available on Kiva.org over the coming months. As stability began to return, Kiva focused resources on areas where it could do the most good—and data helped its leaders make those decisions. "This moment is exactly what Kiva was made for," Matthew says.

THE AMERICAN DREAM IN THE TIME OF COVID-19

For Namgyal Ponsar, the co-owner of the Little Tibet restaurant in Madison, Wisconsin, the COVID-19 crisis brought uncertainty and fear. In addition to the restaurant, she, her brother, and her brother-in-law own two food trucks, which they had to mothball. The restaurant stayed open for takeout in the afternoons and evenings. Revenues declined by 60 percent.

They had borrowed $10,000 from 173 lenders through Kiva when they opened the restaurant in February of 2019. The loan, which carried no interest charges, paid for a walk-in cooler. Before the crisis, Namgyal tucked away five months of repayment funds in her PayPal account to make sure she would stay current on the loan payments. After the crisis struck, she sent an email blast to her lenders telling them how the business was surviving. Several of them sent words of encouragement.

People in Madison have been generous, too. Her landlord decreased her rent, and people she doesn't know called and said they wanted to order takeout—to help her and her family.

Namgyal and her family were refugees. She lived for eight years in a refugee camp in India—where she worked as a farm laborer. She came to the United States on a temporary work permit, trained as a nurse, and eventually became a citizen. She works mornings in a state rehabilitation facility and cooks at the restaurant in the afternoons.

She has worked hard and achieved her American dream, thanks in part to Kiva and her lenders. "I'm very grateful to Kiva," she says. "They're vital for people like us: immigrants who lack funding, networks, and knowledge. It's a platform to help us to get a start and pursue our dreams."

PART 3

THE FUTURE
OF THE
DATA CLOUD

17

DIGITAL TRANSFORMATION

WHEN SNOWFLAKE co-founder Thierry Cruanes was growing up in Normandy, an agricultural region in the north of France, he was a ravenous reader. At 12, he was reading philosophy and history books that were aimed at sophisticated adults. Computers were not on his radar. This was the early 1980s. Then he spotted a personal computer at a local farm fair and was immediately hooked. "I started reading crazy books about what the future would be," Thierry says.

One book in particular caught his fancy. It was about a then-theoretical field of computer science called artificial neural networks. The author predicted that someday computer scientists would design computer systems based on the architecture of the mammal brain—and those computers would be able to learn from interactions with data. To Thierry, this claim seemed far-fetched and supremely exciting at the same time.

Well, that future has arrived, and Thierry is the chief technology officer of a company that manages huge amounts of data—teeing it up for machine-learning algorithms and other artificial intelligence technologies.

The years since Thierry's youth have brought major breakthroughs in computer science and electronics. Some of the most consequential and practical advances have come in the past decade—during Snowflake's lifespan. Those include innovations in artificial intelligence, sensors, cryptography, data management tools, networking, high-performance computing, and quantum computing. Some of these developments are having a huge impact in the here and now, including AI; others, including quantum computing, will be felt more intensely in the coming years.

Taken together, these advances have brought us to a moment in history that seems likely to match the importance of the Industrial Revolution. Already, these new technologies are reshaping the contours of businesses and industries, and they're beginning to reshape the economy and society. It's a digital transformation on a planetary scale.

Data is the beating heart of this moment. More data and more types of data are available now than ever before. Many of these technologies have as their end purpose the harvesting of knowledge from data so enterprises, governments, and the other institutions of society can more effectively fulfill their missions and so humans can live more satisfying and productive lives.

Cloud computing plays a major role in digital transformation. Increasingly, much of the computing in the world is being done in vast cloud data centers operated by Amazon, Microsoft, Google, and others. Everyone—from the CEO of the largest corporation to the schoolteacher down the street—can tap into the cloud to get their work done. It's like an electric power utility.

The cloud is a very big deal for data. It's the optimal place for data to be stored and managed, and for data processing to be done—available, efficient, and affordable.

Which brings us again to the phenomenon of the Data Cloud. Only in the past few years have organizations been able to manage vast quantities and types of data in the cloud. Snowflake's founders reinvented the database for the cloud. That required some impressive engineering. Now the company's computer scientists and engineers are innovating aggressively to extend the core cloud data platform so it does more for customers and so it does more to support innovation by technology partners.

When Thierry looks into the future of the Data Cloud, he sees two major pathways for innovation.

The first is automation. Today, many of the data management and data analytics tasks that are performed on cloud data platforms are manual. They require highly skilled professionals using a variety of sophisticated tools and programming languages to ingest and transform data, manage it, reformat it, query it, and analyze it. In a large number of business scenarios—routine ones where tactical choices are made—these activities and interventions can be automated. Using a combination of artificial intelligence technologies and other computer science approaches, business processes can be virtualized.

Instead of having humans manage a business process and make numerous decisions along the way, all of this can be handled programmatically. You set up a system for managing a process, and then let it run. For instance, in a factory, data can be gathered to monitor a manufacturing process from end to end. Machine-learning algorithms spot anomalies in the data that might signal problems or inefficiencies in the process. When problems are identified, adjustments are made automatically to improve the process.

You can imagine similar scenarios concerning the way we as individuals live our lives. Say you are a 55-year-old man. You're a bit thick around the middle. Your blood pressure is high. You are pre-diabetic. Using the tools of the Internet of Things, we can monitor all these conditions in real time. When your glucose levels suddenly plummet, you can be prompted by your smartphone to eat a candy bar. When your blood pressure rises to a troubling level and stays there for days, your doctor gets an alert. Seconds later, you get a text message from Doc telling you to pick up a new prescription at the pharmacy. If there is evidence that your heart is failing, a message goes directly to an emergency medical unit, which rushes to your location to save your life.

In these scenarios, humans must be taken out of the process as much as possible. They create bottlenecks. They cause delays. They make mistakes. "Humans can't be in the loop anymore," says Thierry. "Their activities produce the data. They consume insights taken from the data. But they can't be in the decision loop."

The second pathway for innovation is providing more powerful tools to help people extract insights from data. In many cases, these activities can't be fully automated. You really need humans in the loop.

A variety of highly skilled professionals make their livings by feasting on data. They include the data engineers who manipulate data and data scientists who use sophisticated techniques to solve complex problems and predict what will happen in the future. They also include business analysts who bridge between data science and marketing or finance.

Thierry believes we will see advances in technology that will help data scientists and data engineers become even better at their jobs. At the same time, advances will come that put data science capabilities in the hands of analysts and even business-unit managers—the so-called citizen data scientists.

Many of these improvements will come from technology partners rather than from Snowflake itself. Snowflake will support its technology partners by adding features to the cloud data platform. "We're part of the revolution, but it's also happening all around us," Thierry says.

The list of Snowflake's technology partners is long. Dozens of companies have built their cloud services on top of Snowflake's platform, and hundreds of them use the platform as a strategically important ingredient in their services.

Next, we highlight a handful of companies that are doing amazing things in the Data Cloud. They are: Matillion, which produces tools for ingesting and transforming data; White Ops, which attacks fraud on digital advertising platforms; Zepl, which provides analytics tools for data scientists; and DataRobot, which brings powerful machine-learning capabilities to the new breed of citizen data scientists.

MATILLION

Based in Denver and Manchester, England, Matillion is a specialist in moving data from its original sources into a cloud data warehouse and preparing it so it's ready for analysis. The company launched in 2011 with the idea of creating business intelligence tools for the cloud, but the founders quickly became frustrated with the existing data-preparation tools, which had not been designed for the cloud. They decided to make better ones—tools that were particularly good at blending a variety of data types in the cloud. Starting in 2015, that became their core business.

During the pre-cloud era, when organizations ran data warehouses in their own data centers, they typically used a process called ETL (Extract, Transform, Load) in which data is extracted from multiple sources, reformatted on the fly, and loaded into the data warehouse. Matillion reengineered ETL for the cloud. Now it's innovating with a different approach, ELT (Extract, Load, Transform). In this scenario, the data is reformatted after it arrives in its more permanent home. Because modern cloud data platforms like Snowflake's are fast, cost-effective, and easy to set up and scale, it makes sense to do the data transformation in the cloud.

Matillion's technologies are designed to make the process simpler, faster, and less expensive. "We call what we do data transformation," says Matthew Scullion, the company's CEO. "It's a business imperative that every company needs to be able to compete using data. Matillion helps you do that faster."

Matillion is a Snowflake customer, but more importantly, the two companies are partners. Many of Matillion's own customers chose to put their data in Snowflake's cloud data platform—where they use Matillion's tools to transform it into the formats that are most useful to them. Matillion's and Snowflake's technologies are designed to work well together.

Typically, a customer will use Matillion's products to ingest data continuously from a variety of sources, remove duplicative or faulty information, combine data of different types, and format so it's easily accessed by analysts. In addition, the products are tuned to work with Snowflake, so, for instance, an analyst can choose the best way to use the technology based on factors including how much data she is processing, and how fast she wants the results.

Matthew sees three trends that are driving the company's product road map. A key focus remains on increasing the sophistication of the tools aimed at the company's current users, the data engineers and data scientists. A second focus is making it easy for customers to see and manage their data even when it is stored and running in more than one public cloud. A third is making the products even easier to use so people within their customers' organizations who aren't computer scientists can curate data so it fits their needs.

For instance, one Matillion customer is in the biotech business—doing research to develop new molecules for medicine, materials science, and green technology. People with PhDs in robotics, biochemistry, and molecular biology are able to use Matillion's products, rather than depending on data engineers to do the work for them. "We think of them as building data warehouses in the cloud," Matthew says. "They think of themselves as doing what they're actually doing—saving the planet and fighting cancer."

WHITE OPS

We're all familiar with CAPTCHA technologies that help websites figure out if they're interacting with a human or a bot. They present puzzles that are easy for humans to solve but difficult for simple bots—distorted letters that you have to decipher and images you have to match. The challenge with most CAPTCHA technologies is that sophisticated bots that look and act like humans can easily outsmart them. The cybersecurity firm White Ops has taken the process of distinguishing between bots and humans to a whole other level of sophistication. It uses advanced algorithms and a multi-layered detection methodology to verify the humanity of more than 1 trillion online interactions every day, protecting many of the largest Internet platforms and enterprises across the globe.

Sophisticated bot fraud has many personalities. Bots look and act like humans when they fill out forms, take over personal accounts, and commit credit card fraud. One of the scams, ad fraud, is largely unknown to the general public, but it may be one of the most damaging.

Every time a person or a bot clicks on a Web page or mobile app where there are ads, money changes hands. Digital advertising is a $300 billion global industry. Fraudsters cheat in a couple ways. In one scenario, they collaborate with unscrupulous website operators and use bots to make millions of false impressions—then split the payments from brands with their co-conspirators. In other cases, they counterfeit popular websites and then drive bot traffic to the fakes. These schemes are possible because a large percentage of digital advertising transactions are done using entirely automated processes. It's like program trading on the stock market. The machines that handle the buying and selling and placing of ads are really fast but can be fooled by sophisticated bot attacks.

Here's where White Ops comes in. It monitors activities by attaching virtual sensors to Web pages and advertisements, looking for signs that indicate a bot, rather than a human, is involved. White Ops' bot mitigation platform is based on a military doctrine, OODA, which stands for Observe, Orient, Decide, and Act. Sometimes they poke bots just to see how they react. Meanwhile, White Ops constantly evolves its own tactics, so hackers are unaware they are being observed. By spotting sophisticated bots quickly and disrupting them, White Ops makes it difficult for ad fraudsters to make money. They go and bother somebody else. "Our core mission is to protect the integrity of the Internet by disrupting the economics of cybercrime," says White Ops CEO Tamer Hassan.

Sometimes, White Ops helps law enforcement agencies catch fraudsters. For instance, in 2017 the company uncovered the 3ve bot network, which had taken over 1.7 million PCs and was using them to launch billions of bot exploits per day. The discovery led eventually to thirteen people being arrested and prosecuted.

White Ops' work is extremely data intensive. When you're tracking a trillion interactions a day, you need a big data warehouse. White Ops uses Snowflake's platform. In fact, it was Snowflake's second customer. Today, White Ops is the global leader in bot mitigation, even though it has just 150 employees. White Ops loads terabytes of data into its Snowflake data platform every day. Its customers get feedback on a particular event in about five milliseconds, and its computing systems know whether to count an interaction as human or to protect against it if it is a bot.

White Ops' bot mitigation platform monitors activities and protects against attacks from across the domains of online advertising, marketing, and application security. That gives the company an incredibly broad view of the nefarious activities on the Internet. White Ops can see patterns in data that others can't. That's one of the reasons the company in early 2020 formed the Satori Threat Intelligence and Research Group, a team of seventy experts dedicated to researching the threats organizations face from the most sophisticated bot attacks. The group shares the information it gathers with all their clients and the wider business community.

White Ops plays the long game against Black Hats, and cloud data analytics is giving the good guys a competitive advantage.

ZEPL

In 2012, when Snowflake's founders were sketching out ideas on a whiteboard in a cramped apartment in San Mateo, the *Harvard Business Review* published an article titled "Data Scientist: The Sexiest Job of the 21st Century." Its authors were Thomas Davenport and D.J. Patil, who later went on to become chief data scientist of the U.S. Office of Science and Technology Policy. In the article, the authors defined a data scientist as "a high-ranking professional with the training and curiosity to make discoveries in the world of big data." They warned that a shortage of people with these skills could constrain the growth of the economy.

This wasn't the origin of the term "data science." It was identified as a new scientific discipline—a combination of mathematics, statistics, and computer science—in the 1990s. But the HBR article came at a turning point. Big Data analytics and Hadoop were all the rage, and there was a rush within tech companies to recruit data scientists. That phenomenon quickly spread to large corporations, and then to smaller organizations. Today, data scientists are sexier than they ever imagined they would be in their wildest dreams.

Data scientists help derive value out of massive amounts of data to provide critical information and insights for businesses, governments, and other organizations. They use a mix of data engineering, statistical analysis, and machine-learning techniques to create analytical applications and to analyze data. You see the use of machine learning in the recommendation engines at companies like Netflix and Amazon, or the automated fraud detection systems used by financial services institutions.

Zepl, a Snowflake partner, provides data science and analytic tools that enable data scientists to reveal this hidden information and insights within vast amounts of data stored in Snowflake's data platform and beyond. Zepl and Snowflake allow enterprises to do this in a secure, scalable, and collaborative fashion so they can adjust quickly to rapidly changing business dynamics and predict the best path forward.

"These technologies enable organizations to combine the best of human and machine intelligence in ways that neither could do as well on its own," says Dan Maloney, Zepl's CEO.

The name Zepl pays homage to its lineage within the Apache Zeppelin open source data science notebook project. The company was launched after users of Zeppelin started clamoring for a commercial, enterprise-scale version of the technology. Moon Lee, the creator of Apache Zeppelin and co-founder of Zepl, helped recruit Dan as CEO in 2018. Shortly after joining Zepl, Dan identified the benefit that Snowflake would bring for more than half a million Apache Zeppelin and Zepl users across the globe.

A lot of Zepl's customers are also Snowflake customers. One customer, for example, uses Zepl and Snowflake to help large brands spot inauthentic news, fake reviews, and hidden groups who control and amplify false narratives. The customer ingests more than 200 million records per day from social media into its Snowflake warehouse. Using machine-learning techniques, it is able to run programs that look for anomalies and detect fakes created by bots and individuals—and take corrective action.

Another Zepl customer captures data from its electric cars, which send back millions of data points every few minutes, to help with predictive maintenance and improved driver safety.

Snowflake's and Zepl's technologies are designed to work well together. For instance, if a data scientist is running machine-learning models on a large quantity of data and she is getting subpar results, she can use Zepl's tools to explore how the models interacted with specific datasets and then debug the datasets or their algorithms.

Dan expects to see data science notebooks becoming ever more powerful and automated. He anticipates being able to create catalogs of metadata about machine-learning models and queries that have been used successfully. All the work done by data analysts in an organization can be tracked and evaluated, and the best work can be identified and turned into reusable modules. Then, whenever somebody in the organization launches a data science project, they can select items from the catalog. "The next time," says Dan, "you don't have to start with a blank notebook. You can be 70 percent of the way there."

DATAROBOT

In 2010, the film *The Social Network* caused a stir across the globe. The tale of the beginnings of Facebook gave many people their first-ever view into the excitement of launching a potentially world-transforming startup and the possibilities that venture capital investment affords. For DataRobot CEO Jeremy Achin, who was then working in the data analytics department of a giant insurance company, the film was both a revelation and a cause for despair. He wanted to be part of something more meaningful. He wanted to invent something and to make a real impact on the world.

Back at the insurance company, Jeremy took a closer look at how he and his colleagues were doing their work. For every predictive analytics application they developed, they spent months designing and writing thousands of lines of software code. They bought specialized analytics tools and algorithms from tiny tech startups and stitched them together. Then they went to the company's IT department to get the computing resources they needed and tested the applications. Finally, if they were lucky, the model they designed went into production. The whole process might take a year to eighteen months, and, in many cases, projects never made it into production and, thus, were nothing more than glorified science experiments.

There had to be a better way, he thought.

At the same time, three major trends in computing were starting to take off: the Big Data explosion, cloud computing, and major advances in artificial intelligence. Jeremy saw the opportunity to take advantage of these developments and build a company that could automate the manual and time-intensive process of developing data analytics applications.

In 2012, Jeremy and one of his co-workers, Tom de Godoy, founded DataRobot. (Tom is the CTO.) The goal was to develop a flexible platform that would automate the machine learning process to allow enterprises to build highly accurate predictive models in a fraction of the time, in whatever deployment environment worked best for customers (cloud or on-premises). They would transform both business analysts who lacked software programming and AI skills into "citizen data scientists" and more advanced data scientists into "super data scientists."

Automating the end-to-end process was no easy feat. The product spent years in development before hitting the market in 2015. Still, they were way ahead of the competition. Their targets ranged from data scientists and business analysts to IT professionals, software developers, and even business executives. Executives don't do the actual analytics— rather, they use the platform to get an overview of all the projects across their organizations.

DataRobot's founders had built a product that incorporates computer science, statistics, and data science knowledge into an intuitive, automated, end-to-end platform. Users point the platform at a single dataset or collection of datasets and pick a goal that they want to achieve. The DataRobot technology then chooses the most appropriate components from many different data sources and machine learning algorithms— developing multiple "blueprints" or selecting one that has already been developed. The platform then creates highly accurate predictive models. Finally, when the models are being used, the platform continuously monitors them to optimize their performance. DataRobot's technology compresses what might normally be a one-year process into a matter of days.

A large grocery store chain, for instance, can use the platform for demand forecasting. The company might have 3,000 stores and 60,000 products per store. The platform helps them more accurately predict how many of each item they should stock in each individual store based on local sales records combined with other data. That way they have the inventory they need on hand but not more than they need.

In many cases, the datasets that DataRobot's technology uses to train the models are stored and managed in Snowflake's cloud data platform. The two companies' technologies are tuned to work well together.

Looking forward several years, Jeremy foresees massive changes coming for how humans and machines collaborate to make decisions across the enterprise. He describes a four-level hierarchy of methods for making decisions. It starts with people deciding based on their intuition, unaided by data. A lot of leaders use this approach, even today. Second, data and business intelligence tools come into play. Then, next level up, humans make decisions aided by artificial intelligence. That's becoming routine in enterprises. In the future, Jeremy expects machines to make many of our decisions for us, at first monitored and evaluated closely by humans but eventually operating more and more independently.

Jeremy sees machine learning becoming ubiquitous in enterprises— applied to practically everything an organization does and every decision it makes. "We think there will be trillions of AI use cases by 2025 or so," he says. "That's only possible if this view of machine intelligence and automation actually happens. There's no way that data scientists will be able to manually build that many AI models, monitor and keep track of them, and make sure they're healthy. It all has to be automated."

DATA IS POWER

FRANK SLOOTMAN

HAD BEEN WORKING in the software business for more than thirty years when I took the job as CEO of Snowflake a year ago. By now, I know my way around enterprise software. Most recently, I spent six years at the helm of ServiceNow, a Software-as-a-Service company. That's enterprise software hosted in the cloud. So I know my way around the SaaS world, too. But, until I landed at Snowflake, I didn't fully appreciate the real power of data. In fact, I now believe that *data is power.*

Data is the new way of seeing and interpreting the world. When handled right, it's more trustworthy than our five senses, our reason, and our memories. It enables us to understand what's happening around us with more clarity, scale, precision, and certainty; to understand causation; to move faster; and to see into the future. In a data-powered organization, facts and insights augment and often trump opinions and instincts.

These days, there is no more critical factor in the success or failure of a company, or any other organization, than its ability to extract signals from data and put data to work at scale.

What makes all this possible is the rise of the Data Cloud. Over the past decade and a half, cloud computing emerged as the most significant force in the computer industry. It's disrupting not only the tech industry but also business, government, and the economy. In the early years of the cloud revolution, there were two major paradigm shifts. One was the public cloud, which frees enterprises from having to buy and manage their own computers. The second was SaaS, buying software on a subscription basis. But now we're seeing a third element—the mass migration of data to the cloud. I believe that this shift will compound the two that came before.

Many enterprises and government agencies aren't just moving to the cloud—they are moving their data to cloud data platforms like Snowflake's. There, it can be managed, analyzed, and governed in much more effective ways. In the Dark Ages of computing, enterprises locked their data away in databases controlled by the people who gathered it, making it difficult for anybody else in the organization to gain access. Data was stuck. A cloud data platform puts all your data in one place so it's easier to discover, share, and analyze. A cloud data platform mobilizes data so you can improve business processes and make better decisions. These technologies enable organizations to be truly data driven.

The power of data started to become clear to me in my early days at Snowflake. We have a regular email blast called Deal Updates that employees can subscribe to. The data comes out of our Salesforce CRM software. Sales managers pick some of the top wins, and the reps who closed those deals write up detailed descriptions of what they sold, who they beat, and how the customer is using the technology. After I joined the company, I read these updates religiously and I would sometimes be shocked by how powerful the technology was.

Customers were seeing tremendous improvements in processing performance. A task that used to take twenty minutes now took twenty seconds. The technology was producing orders-of-magnitude improvements. At the same time, the platform was able to handle huge stores of data. We're talking petabyte scale. This meant that Snowflake was breaking two boundaries at once—the sheer scale of the data and the immense amount of computing power brought to bear on it. There's a simple formula: Volume plus velocity equals competitive advantage. This is what you get when you have a data platform built from scratch to run at cloud scale.

Everybody talks about Big Data these days, but the term doesn't do justice to the opportunity that we have before us. The term typically refers to all the unstructured and semi-structured data that is being pulled into enterprise data management systems from Internet of Things sensors, smartphones, and social media.

I think it makes more sense to just talk about data with a small "d." Data comes in all sizes and types. By expanding the scope of our thinking, we rope in all the normal stuff that organizations collect in their relational databases, plus data they purchase from others. Yes, we need computing systems that can handle tremendous volumes of data. But we also need systems that can ingest all kinds of data and then transform it into usable formats, integrate it, manage it, analyze it, and most of all: act on it.

THE RISE OF THE CLOUD DATA PLATFORM

A cloud data platform does all those things. Snowflake started off with a sharp focus on reinventing the data warehouse for the cloud. I credit co-founders Benoit Dageville and Thierry Cruanes and their original engineering team with tearing up the old data management bible and writing a new one. Now they're expanding our cloud data platform. It's a much bigger idea. They're innovating like mad again. At the same time, we're connecting with a host of technology companies, data providers, and IT services partners, so, together, we can offer customers a complete integrated environment where they can handle all things data.

One of the chief benefits of using a cloud data platform is that it enables enterprises to fully automate many of their core business processes. Data that comes from transactions, IoT devices, the Internet, and internal operations triggers actions programmatically. No humans need be involved. If you change jobs, your resignation prompts all the processes that are required to leave one company and join another. In a factory, all the data that comes off machine sensors streams into a data warehouse where it can be interpreted and acted on—producing continuous improvements to the manufacturing process.

This is a machine-to-machine business. It takes the human out of the loop, which makes the process more efficient, massively scalable, and less prone to error. In the past, systems supported people. Now, it's the other way around. People are supporting systems.

There are numerous other benefits from a cloud data platform, as well.

SPEED MATTERS: Everybody with a passing acquaintance with Wall Street knows about a concept called the time value of money. It's the idea that money available now is more valuable than the identical sum at some time in the future because of its earning capacity. There's a parallel concept in the data world: the time value of data. Information is more valuable when it arrives rapidly and can be acted on at once. The longer it takes for data to arrive and process, the less valuable it becomes.

A cloud data platform speeds the flow from data gathering to insight and to action. In some cases, data streams directly from its sources into the data platform and then into enterprises' real-time computing systems—enabling, for instance, a pizza restaurant chain to change the time of delivery when a pizza is still in the oven after a customer texts that they're delayed in traffic. It also keeps data fresh. The ability to share data instantly means, for instance, that sales and marketing information can be continuously updated and acted on to improve the results of a marketing campaign.

DATA SHARING FUELS THE DATA ECONOMY: The ability to quickly and readily share information—both internally and with partners—is critical for the modern enterprise. A cloud data platform enables diverse business organizations to share data instantly, securely, and with no potential for shared information to be used improperly or to become out of date.

We've talked about the power of data network effects. The more organizations share data, the more value that data provides to each of the parties involved. The cloud data platform creates a vast network of data sharers. The more participants in the platform and the more data they store, the more value is created for all of them. They can get clearer views of what's happening in the world, and they can collaborate with one another in ways that were not possible before.

In the twentieth century, many enterprises sought to become vertically integrated so they could operate more efficiently. But it also meant they became monolithic and bureaucratic and were slow to react to changes in the business environment. The cloud data platform enables organizations to remain lean and focused—and to interact with their lean and focused business partners with a minimum of friction and a maximum of alignment.

MARKETPLACES FOR THE DATA ECONOMY: Again, think back to the early days of the twentieth century. That's when a few dozen traders were buying and selling securities in a small building on Broad Street in downtown Manhattan. Now, look at equities markets today. The average daily trading value on the New York Stock Exchange tops $200 billion. The data exchanges that are being established today have the potential to operate on a billion-dollar scale. Any organization can offer its data for sale to other organizations, which can combine it with other data to create added value.

You can imagine a future where data exchanges offer for sale all the assets and tools that an enterprise needs to thrive in the data economy—not just datasets but analytics tools and machine-learning algorithms tailored for every business purpose. Data exchanges have the potential to become one-stop shops for data and the tools and expertise to exploit data.

HOW TO BECOME A DATA-DRIVEN COMPANY

Snowflake itself is a data-driven company, of course. We use our own instance of our cloud data platform, which we call Snowhouse, to run nearly every aspect of the business. That includes everything from finance, to marketing, to engineering, to sales.

Many of our customers are data driven, as well. That's especially true of the digital-native and cloud-native companies that were among our early customers. I'm thinking of companies like DoorDash, which delivers meals from restaurants, and KIXEYE, a gaming company focused on mobile and online gaming markets. Everything they do is fueled by data and managed with automated digital processes. We're also starting to see rapid uptake among advertising, marketing, and financial services companies. For instance, Coatue, a hedge fund, is shifting much of its data consumption to the cloud.

But other companies we meet with are all over the map. Some are still operating with mainframes or old-fashioned client-server computing setups. They have just barely begun to shift their data into the cloud. Others have committed to making the transition, but they're bumping into all sorts of organizational and cultural impediments.

We see this especially among healthcare, education, and government organizations. Often, it is the IT executives who are reluctant to abandon technologies and computing models in which they have invested a lot of time and money. They are understandably risk-averse, but as time wears on that posture holds everybody back.

I believe that there's equal risk in going slowly. Time is not your friend. If your competitors get to the Data Cloud picnic first, they will eat your lunch.

The migration to the Data Cloud has been slow going, but it is picking up speed. Everybody is running out of excuses, and the promise of scale, performance, and efficiency beckons.

The top leaders in an enterprise have to make the commitment and set the tone. This is tough for people in the C-suite, including the CEO and the CFO. They don't typically have a technology background, and, god knows, cloud computing and data science are complex topics. But the first step for companies is to get educated, to become proficient. A huge shift is happening right now, and they better get on it. A static mindset is not helpful. Change is constant and inevitable. Organizations need to build the muscle to adopt to wave after wave of technology. The further you get behind the curve, the harder it is to catch up.

The next step is hiring the right sort of people with the right outlook and skills. It's common now to see all kinds of new titles in the C-suite: for instance, chief digital officer, chief data officer, and chief transformation officer. It all reflects a desire to establish organization ownership of change.

The CFO has to understand how data creates value and how data monetization might become a new revenue stream for an enterprise. The CIO, often the most reluctant person in the room, has to buy in, of course. If your current CIO is fighting the move to the cloud, it might be time for that person to move on.

In addition, you need people with new skill sets deeper in the organization. Hire data scientists—people who use machine-learning algorithms and modern programming languages to do more sophisticated data analytics. You need data engineers who know how to curate data and to transform it into forms that are more accessible. Then you need to train your front-line business leaders to learn how to use data analytics. They need to get answers quickly, and they should not depend on data analysts and data scientists to do everything for them.

The next step is adopting a richly featured cloud data platform—one that you can build your data-driven business on. Snowflake is one option. There are others working to meet the challenge. The market is already sorting the ones that work and the ones that do not.

I'm optimistic when I look into the future. Data is power. Data is moving to the cloud. A cloud data platform is where all this great work can take place. Ultimately, we may have much of the data the world produces essentially in one place—effectively one giant database for the entire planet to tap into. That's when things get really interesting. The potential for improving the lives of individuals, the effectiveness of organizations, and the dynamism of the global economy is limitless. Let's go there.

COMPANY INDEX

COMPANY INDEX